BV
V501
M87
981

ИOITƆƎ⅃
⅃ƆƎ⅃Ǝ

Brengle Memorial Library
The s...
...y
...aining

THE INNER CHAMBER

S E L E C T

C O L L E C T I O N

Minister's Library
1986

THE NUDE
CHAMBER

THE INNER CHAMBER

Andrew Murray

Contemporized
by
Leona F. Choy

CHRISTIAN LITERATURE CRUSADE
Fort Washington, Pennsylvania 19034

CHRISTIAN LITERATURE CRUSADE
Fort Washington, Pennsylvania 19034

CANADA
Box 189, Elgin, Ontario KOG 1EO

GREAT BRITAIN
51 The Dean, Alresford, Hants., SO24 9BJ

AUSTRALIA
P. O. Box 91, Pennant Hills, N.S.W. 2120

Copyright © 1981
Leona Frances Choy

This Edition 1981
This Printing 1985

ISBN 0-87508-405-2

All Rights Reserved. No part of this publication may be
translated, reproduced, or transmitted in any form or by
any means, electronic or mechanical, including photo-
copy, recording, or any information storage and retrieval
system, without permission in writing from the publisher.

PRINTED IN THE UNITED STATES OF AMERICA

CONTENTS

PREFACE

The Inner Chamber suggests thoughts of the utmost importance: the daily need to come apart from other people and be quiet; the true spirit of prayer; the devotional reading of God's Word; and fellowship with God. The quiet time is meant to strengthen our spiritual life and prepare us for daily responsibilities. It makes us ready to serve in God's kingdom by interceding for people and winning them to the Lord. Of all the times of the day, our secret time with the Lord should be our source of joy and strength.

I have not attempted to put the thoughts in this book systematically, but I hope the fragments I have given may help cultivate your hidden inner life and your communion with God.

In South Africa there are various diseases that affect our orange trees. One of them is popularly known as root disease. A tree may continue to bear some fruit and an ordinary observer may not notice anything wrong. But an expert sees the beginning of a slow death. A similar disease affects the roots in the vineyards. The only way to eliminate this disease is a radical one of taking out the old roots and providing new ones. A former branch of the vine is grafted on an American root, and in due time you have the same stem and branches as before; but *the roots are new* and able to resist the disease. The disease comes in that part of the plant that is *hidden from sight* and that is where healing must be sought

How the Church of Christ and the spiritual life of thousands of its members suffers from the root disease! It is none other than the neglect of secret communion with God. It is the lack of private prayer, the neglect of maintaining our hidden spiritual life *"rooted* in Christ," *"rooted* and grounded in love," that explains the weakness of the Christian life. No wonder we can't resist the world. No wonder we fail to bring forth fruit abundantly. Nothing can change this except restoring the quiet time with the Lord in the life of the believer. We must give it the place which Christ meant it to have. As Christians, we must learn not to trust our own efforts but to daily sink our roots deeper into Christ and to make the secret personal fellowship with God our priority. Then true godliness will flourish. *If the root be holy, so are the branches.* If the morning hour is kept holy for the Lord, the whole day with its duties will be, too. Healthy roots grow healthy branches.

Most of these chapters appeared first as articles in THE SOUTH AFRICAN PIONEER. Some who were helped by reading them urged me to have them published, which was done by the South Africa General Mission. I pray that God may bless them to some of His children in the pursuit of the deeper and more fruitful life, the life hid with Christ in God.

Andrew Murray

1

THE MORNING HOUR

*"My voice shalt Thou hear in the morning,
O Lord; in the morning will I direct my
prayer unto Thee, and will look up."*
(Psalms 5:3)
*"The Lord God wakeneth morning by
morning, He wakeneth mine ear to hear as
they that are taught."* (Isaiah 50:4)

From the earliest ages God's people have
thought of the morning as the time especially
appropriate for the worship of God. It is still
regarded by Christians both as a duty and a privilege to set aside some portion of the beginning of
the day to seek quiet and fellowship with God.
Some have termed it The Morning Watch, others
the Quiet Hour or the Quiet Time. Whether it is a
full sixty minutes or only a portion of an hour, the
motivation is the same: to unite with the Psalmist
when he says, "My voice shalt Thou hear in the
morning, O Lord."

In pointing out the extreme importance of such
a daily time of quiet for prayer and meditation on
God's Word, Dr. John R. Mott has said, "Next to
receiving Christ as Saviour, and claiming the filling
of the Holy Spirit, we know of no act attended with
larger good to ourselves or others than the forma-

tion of an undiscourageable resolution to keep the morning watch and spend the first half hour of the day alone with God."

At first that statement may seem to appear too strong. The act of receiving Christ as Saviour is one of such infinite consequence for eternity, and the experience of being filled with the Holy Spirit is one that works such a revolution in the Christian life, that such a simple thing as the firm determination to keep the morning watch hardly appears important enough to be placed next to them. However, when we think how impossible it is to live our daily life in Christ and be kept from sin, or to maintain a walk in the leading and power of the Holy Spirit, without daily, close fellowship with God, we shall soon see that this statement is not exaggerated. By this simple daily act we express that we have a fixed determination that Christ shall have our whole lives and that we will fully obey the Holy Spirit in everything. The morning watch is the key to unceasingly and fully maintaining our surrender to Christ.

What is the purpose of the morning watch? (We shall henceforth use this term to refer to a time set aside daily for the cultivation of our communion with God.) It is not to be an end in itself. Nor is it enough that we have a profitable time from our prayer and Bible study and then come forth with some measure of refreshment and help. It is a means to an end. The goal is to secure the presence of Christ for the whole day. Personal devotion to Jesus means that we do not allow anything to separate us from Him for a moment. To one who is truly devoted to Him, it cannot possibly be an intermittent thing to abide in Him and His love, to be kept by Him and do His will and please Him. The hymns, *I Need Thee Every Hour* and *Moment by Moment I'm Kept in His Love,* are the language of life and truth. "In Thy name shall they rejoice all the day" and "I the Lord do keep it; I will water it every moment" are words of power. The believer cannot stand for one moment without Christ. If we are personally devoted to Him, we can't be satisfied unless we are always abiding in His love and His will. This is the true scriptural Christian life that makes the morning watch so vital.

When we are convinced that our success for the day depends on our seeking and finding and holding Him in our morning watch, we will allow nothing to interfere with it. It will be the means to this great end. Meditation, prayer and reading the Word will be subordinate to laying hold of the presence of Christ. The morning watch is the link for the day between Christ and me which must be renewed and firmly fastened in the morning hour. At first, we may be afraid that the cares and pleasures and temptations of the whole day may crush the benefit we have enjoyed in our quiet time. Don't be disturbed about that. Christ is forming His character in us and gradually, in our most commonplace actions, He will show Himself through us. It takes time. Whether we are relaxing or involved in the business of life, it shall eventually become second nature to us to act according to the spirit and the will of Christ. All this can be because Christ, Himself, as the Living One, lives in us and is not separated from us. If we truly recognize this, we will never be able to speak of walking outside of His presence as we leave the morning watch.

Don't let it bother you if it seems to be too high or difficult a goal or occupies too much of your quiet time at first to secure the living presence of God. The reward is rich. The effect this will begin to have on your day will be to give it new meaning and power.

This will also have an effect on the spirit in which you keep the morning watch. When your purpose is to have a definite conscious meeting with Christ upon each occasion, and secure His presence for the day, you will fix your determination. Whatever effort or self-denial it may cost you will be worth it to win that prize. If the same single-minded determination is expected in academic study and on the sports field, does not our spiritual life deserve even more intense devotion? Surely the love of Christ needs the whole heart. That will keep you from being superficial or just putting in time. It will strengthen your character and fortify you to say *No* when you face the temptation of self-indulgence. You will come to your quiet time with your whole heart and be at once ready to communicate with Christ. It will establish the keynote of your daily life.

It is said: Great things are possible to any man who knows what he wills and wills it with all his heart. If we come to our morning watch expecting to meet Christ personally, we will not be disappointed. Our faith is rewarded by the presence of Christ waiting to meet us and take charge of us for the day. Let it stir us up to realize that *a living Christ waits to meet us!*

2

THE DOORS SHUT—ALONE WITH GOD

*"When thou prayest, enter into thine inner
chamber, and having shut thy door, pray
to thy Father, which seeth in secret."*
(Matt. 6:6)

Man was created for fellowship with God. To
accomplish this, God made man in His own image
and likeness. He was capable of understanding and
enjoying God, of entering into His will and delighting in His glory. Because God is everywhere and in
everything, man could have lived in the enjoyment
of an unbroken fellowship right in the midst of
whatever work he had to do.

Sin broke up this precious reciprocal fellowship
between God and man.

It remains true that nothing but this fellowship
can satisfy the heart of either man or God. That is
what Christ came to restore—to bring His lost creature back to God, and to bring man back to all that
he was created for. Communion with God is the
highest blessing on earth as well as in heaven. It
becomes a full experience when two statements are
spoken: "I will be with thee, I will never leave thee
nor forsake thee," and when we can say, "The
Father is always with me."

Such communion with God is meant to be ours during the whole day, whatever our condition or circumstances. But its enjoyment depends upon the reality of the communion we have with God in the inner chamber. The power for maintaining close and glad fellowship with God all day will depend largely upon the intensity with which we seek to secure it in the time of secret prayer. The one essential during the morning watch is *fellowship with God*.

It is also our Lord's direct teaching: "Shut thy door and pray to thy Father which seeth in secret." The chief thing to do in secret is to obtain the Father's presence and attention. Know that He sees and hears you. More important than all your urgent requests, or your efforts to pray right, is the child-like, living assurance that *your Father sees you*. You meet Him there, His eyes are on you and yours on Him, and you are now enjoying actual communion with Him.

Christian! There is a terrible danger to which you stand exposed in your inner chamber. You are in danger of substituting prayer and Bible study for living fellowship with God. You may get so occupied with your needs and their expression, your method of praying and believing, that the light of His face and the joy of His love can't even enter you. You might get so interested in your Bible study, and the delightful emotions it arouses in you that—yes—the very Word of God may become a substitute for God Himself. Your soul becomes preoccupied and you do not lead it to God at all. Then you go out into the day's work without the power of an abiding fellowship and wonder why you are so weak in your spirit.

What a difference it would make in the lives of many, if they looked upon that time of morning watch as a definite engagement with the Father and understood that it grieves Him when it is broken. What strength we miss; what daily control by the Father; what preparedness for anything that might come to us when we do not secure God's presence with us through this daily appointment with God.

"Thy Father which seeth in secret will reward thee openly." When the secret fellowship with the Father is experienced and maintained, it will be evident in public—the reward will be there. The Father takes charge and rewards you openly. This is the only sure way to live with people in the power of God's blessing.

3

THE OPEN DOOR—THE OPEN REWARD

"When thou fastest, anoint thine head and wash thy face, that thou appear not unto men to fast, but to thy Father which seeth in secret; and thy Father, which seeth in secret, shall reward thee openly."
(Matt. 6:17, 18)

"When they saw the boldness of Peter and John they took knowledge of them that they had been with Jesus." (Acts 4:13)

"And it came to pass when Moses came down from Mount Sinai, that he wist not that the skin of his face shone while he talked with them. And when Aaron and all the children of Israel saw Moses, behold, the skin of his face shone; and they were afraid to come nigh to him. And till Moses had done speaking with them, he put a veil upon his face." (Exodus 34: 29-33)

The transition from fellowship with God in the morning watch to communication with people is often difficult. If we have truly met God, we want to keep that sense of His presence and our response of surrender to Him. Perhaps we go out to the breakfast table and in the sudden contact with our own family the atmosphere is suddenly changed. As the presence of people and things that are visible assert themselves, we begin to lose what we had found. Many young Christians have been disturbed with the question of how to keep one's heart full of that which you don't even feel free to talk about because it seems so sacred. Even in Christian company it isn't always easy to freely talk about the spiritual things which mean the most to you. We should try to learn how our contacts with people may be a help, instead of a hindrance, in maintaining a life of continual fellowship with God.

The story of Moses with the veil on his face teaches us some lessons. Close and continued fellowship with God will in due time leave an impression on us which others will notice. Moses didn't know that his face shone. The light of God shining from us will be unconscious. If anything, it will serve to deepen the sense of our being an earthen vessel (1 Cor. 2:3,4, and 2 Cor. 4). The sense of God's presence in us may cause other people to feel uncomfortable in our presence. The true believer will not take advantage of this or act more holy, but will know what it means to veil his face and prove by humility and love that he is the same as those around him. And yet, through it all, there will be that proof that he is a child of God who has dealings with the heavenly world.

The same lesson was taught by our Lord about fasting. No show should be made of it; we should meet people in the joy and gentleness of the Lord. You can count upon God, who has seen you in secret. to reward you openly.

The story of Peter and John confirms the same truth. They had been with Jesus while He was on earth, and when He entered heaven they had received His Spirit. They were simply expressing what the Spirit of Christ taught them, and even their enemies could see by their boldness that they had been with Jesus.

The blessing of communion with God is truly very delicate and may easily be lost by entering too deeply into involvements with people. We should keep a holy watchfulness during the day because we don't know when the enemy might come. We should be characterized by a quiet self-restraint and continual looking to the Lord. It is sometimes a help within the Christian family for each one to repeat a Scripture verse at the breakfast table on some particular subject, therefore making it easier to keep the conversation on a spiritual level. As you seek and find the Lord's presence in the morning watch more regularly, gradually you will be able to go on into the day's duties with the continuity of fellowship kept unbroken. It is a great thing to enter the inner chamber and shut the door and meet the Father in secret. It is a greater thing to open the door again and go out in the enjoyment of His presence which nothing can disturb.

Some people do not think that such a life is necessary and feel that the strain is too great. They believe that one can be a good Christian without it. But, it is essential for those who want to be earnest Christians and serve in God's kingdom and influence the world for Christ, to be full of God and His presence. To such it will be all important to know how to carry the heavenly treasure in their earthen vessel and have the power of Christ resting upon them all day.

4

MOSES AND THE WORD OF GOD

*"When Moses was gone into the tabernacle
to speak with God, then he heard the voice
of one speaking to him from off the mercy
seat: and God spake unto him."* (Num. 7:89)

When you pray, you speak to God; when you
read the Bible, God speaks to you. When Moses
went in to pray for himself or his people, and to wait
for instructions, he found that One waiting for him.
What a lesson for the morning watch! A prayerful
spirit is the spirit to which God will speak. A prayerful spirit will be a listening spirit waiting to hear
what God says. In communion with God, His presence and the part He takes must be as real as our
own. How can our Scripture reading and praying
contribute to this true fellowship with God?

First, we should *get into the right place.* As
Moses went into the tabernacle he separated himself
from people. He went where he could be alone and
where God was to be found. Jesus told us where
that place is for us. He told us to enter into our
inner chamber, whatever that represents in our circumstances, shut the door, and pray to our Father
who sees in secret. Anywhere we can really be alone
with God may be for us the secret place of His pres-

ence. To speak with God we need separation from everything else. We need to set our hearts intently upon meeting God personally and fully expect to do so, and have direct dealings with Him. Those who go there to speak to God will hear the voice of One speaking to them.

Next, *get into the right position.* God was speaking to Moses from the mercy seat. To bow before the mercy seat indicates a spirit of humility. We know our own unworthiness and that is a real help in trusting God. We can be sure that our upward look will be met by His eyes, that our prayers will be heard, and that His loving answer will be given. As you bow before the mercy seat, you can be sure that the God of mercy will see and bless you.

And then, *get into the right disposition.* This means the listening attitude. Many of us are so occupied with the much or the little that we have to say in our prayers that the voice of One speaking from the mercy seat is never heard. It is not even expected or waited for. 'Thus saith the Lord,' The heaven is My throne and the earth is My footstool; to this man will I look, even to him that is poor and of a contrite heart, and trembleth at My word.'" We will hear God speak in the Word we read. The highest blessedness of prayer will be when we stop praying and let God speak.

Prayer and the Word are inseparably linked. Power in the use of either depends upon the presence of the other. The Word tells me what to pray about and what God will do for me. It shows me how to pray and how God would have me come to Him. It gives me the power for prayer, the assurance that I will be heard. The Word brings me the answer to prayer because it teaches me what God will do for me. On the other hand, prayer prepares my heart to receive the Word from God Himself, for the teaching of the Spirit to give me spiritual understanding of it, and for the faith that is made partaker of its mighty working.

It is easy to understand why they are inseparable. Prayer and the Word have one common center—God. Prayer seeks God; the Word reveals God. In prayer, man asks God; in the Word, God answers man. In prayer, man rises into the heavenlies to dwell with God; in the Word, God comes to dwell with man. In prayer, man gives himself to God; in the Word, God gives Himself to man. Make God the one object of your desire. Then prayer and the Word will interchange and a blessed fellowship with God will take place. God will dwell in you and you in God. Seek God and live!

5

MOSES—THE MAN OF PRAYER

Following the patriarchal era, Moses was the first man appointed to be a teacher and leader of men. In his life we find wonderful illustrations of the place and power of intercession in a servant of God.

Let us study Moses' prayers. In the wilderness, from his first call, he prayed. He asked God what he was supposed to say to the people (Ex. 3:11-13). He told God all about his weaknesses and requested to be relieved of his mission (Ex. 4:1-13). When the people reproached him that their burdens were unbearable, he told God about it (Ex. 5:22), and he made known to God all his fears (Ex. 6:12). This was his first training in prayer. From such experiences was born his power in prayer when, time after time, Pharaoh asked him to entreat the Lord for him, and deliverance came in answer to Moses' request (Ex. 8:8,9,12,28,29,30,31; 9:28,29,33; 10:17,18). Study these passages until you come under the full impression of how real a factor prayer was in Moses' work and God's redemption.

At the Red Sea Moses cried to God with the people and the answer came (Ex. 14:15). In the wilderness when the people got thirsty, and when Amalek attacked them, it was also prayer that brought deliverance (Ex. 17:4,11).

At Sinai when Israel had made the golden calf, it was prayer that at once averted the threatened destruction (Ex. 32:11,14). It was renewed prayer that gained restoration (Ex.32: 31). It was more prayer that secured God's presence to go with them (Ex. 33:17). Once again, it was prayer that brought the revelation of God's glory (Ex. 33:19), and when that had been given, it was fresh prayer that received the renewal of the covenant (Ex. 34:9,10).

In Deuteronomy we have a wonderful summary of all this (Deut. 9:18,19,20,26). We see with what intensity Moses prayed, and how in one case it was for forty days and forty nights that he fell on his face before the Lord (Deut. 9:25; 10:10).

In Numbers we read of Moses' prayer quenching the fire of the Lord (Num. 11:2), and obtaining the supply of meat (Num. 11:31); of prayer healing Miriam (Num. 12:13); of prayer again saving the nation when they had refused to go up to the land (Num. 14:17-20). Prayer brought down judgment on Korah (Num. 16:15), and when God would have consumed the whole multitude, prayer made atonement (Num. 16:46). Prayer brought water out of the rock (Num. 20:6), and in answer to prayer the brazen serpent was given (Num. 21:7). In answer to prayer God's will was made known in a case of difficulty (Num. 27:5), and Joshua was given as Moses' successor (Num. 27:16).

Study all this until your whole heart is filled with the thought of the part prayer must play and will play in the life of a man who would be God's servant to his fellowmen.

As we study, the parts will unite into a living

whole and Moses will become a living model for our prayer life. We shall learn what is needed to be an intercessor. Here are some of the lessons:

Moses was a man surrendered to God, zealous, even jealous, for God and for His honor and will.

He was a man absolutely given up for the good of his people, ready to sacrifice himself to save them.

Moses was a man conscious of his divine calling to act as the mediator, the link and channel of communication and blessing between God and men on earth. His life was so entirely possessed by this mediatorial consciousness that he simply and naturally expected God would answer his prayers.

We learn from his example that God, in answer to the prayers of one man, saves and blesses those He has entrusted to him and does what He would not otherwise do. We see how the whole government of God has made prayer one of the constituent parts of His plan. We see how prayers from earth are the power that brings God's blessings down from heaven.

Above all we see how prayer is an index of the spiritual life and how its power depends upon our relation to God and the consciousness of being His representative. God entrusts His work to me and the more simple and complete my devotion to His interests, the more natural and certain becomes the assurance that He hears me.

God had the most prominent place in Moses' life: God had sent him; God had promised to be with him; God therefore always helped him when he prayed.

What is the practical application to ourselves?

How shall I learn to pray like Moses? I cannot do it by an act of my will. My first lesson must be to realize that I am weak and incapable of doing so on my own. Then, as I surrender to God's training, slowly and surely I will learn. Though the training will be gradual, one thing I can do at once—I can decide to give myself to this life of prayer and assume the right attitude. Christian, do this now. Make the decision to live entirely as a channel for God's blessing to flow through you to the world. Take the step. If necessary, take ten minutes for deliberate thought. Accept the Divine appointment and start by accepting some object of intercession.

Take time this next week and get a firm hold on the elementary truths that Moses' examples teach. Just as a music teacher insists upon the pupil practicing scales, set your determination to learn thoroughly, starting with those necessary first lessons.

God seeks men through whom He can bless the world. Say definitely, "Here I am. I will give my life to this." Develop your faith in that simple truth that God hears prayer; God will do what you ask.

Give yourself as wholly for the sake of men as you have given yourself to God. Open your eyes to the needs of the world. Take your stand in Christ and in the power which His name and life and Spirit gives you. Start now to practice definite intercession.

6

MOSES—THE MAN OF GOD

"Moses, the man of God, blessed the children of Israel." (Deut. 33:1)

The man of God! How much that term signifies! He is a man who comes from God, is chosen and sent by Him. He is a man who walks with God, lives in His fellowship and carries the mark of His presence. He is a man who lives for God and His will; whose whole being is ruled by the glory of God; who involuntarily and unceasingly leads men to think of God. A man of God is one in whose heart and life God has taken the right place as the All in all, and who has only one desire, that God should have that place of pre-eminence throughout the world.

Such men of God are what the world needs. God is seeking them so that He may fill them with Himself and send them into the world to help others to know Him. Moses was so distinctly such a man, that men naturally spoke of him with that term— Moses, the man of God. Every believer ought to aim at being such a living witness and proof that God can live in men on earth.

The thought of being a person so closely linked to God that others instinctively refer to his chief characteristic as being a man of God, leads us further. It suggests the idea of the impression we make upon men and the power we can have by carrying the holy presence of God with us. How essential men of God are to the world—and to God! God has planned them to be the link between Himself and the world which, by sin, has fallen away from Him. In Christ the world has been redeemed for God. But God has no way of showing men what they ought to be, of awakening, calling and helping them, except through men of God in whom His life, His Spirit and His power are working. Man was created so that God might live, work and show forth His glory in and through him. When the redemption of Christ was completed with the descent of God the Holy Spirit into the hearts of men, this indwelling was restored and God regained possession of His home. Therefore, when a person gives himself up wholly to the presence of the Holy Spirit, not only as a power working in him, but as God Himself dwelling in him, he may become, in the deepest meaning of the word, *a man of God!* (John 14:16,20,23)

Paul tells us that it is through the power of Holy Scripture that *the man of God* is complete. This implies that with some, the life is not complete and needs to be made perfect. "Every scripture is inspired of God, and is profitable for teaching, for reproof, for correction, for instruction in righteousness, that *the man of God* may be complete, furnished completely to every good work."
(2 Tim: 3:16,17)

This brings us again to the morning watch as the

chief time for personal Bible study. As we yield heart and life to the Word, through its teaching, its reproof, its correction, its instruction, we come under the direct operation of God and into full communion with Him. Then the man of God will be complete and equipped for every good work.

Oh! May we have grace to be truly men of God! A man of God knows and proves three things: God is all; God claims all; God works all. Seek to be a man of God! Let God in the morning watch be all to you. Let God during the day be all to you. Let your life be devoted to one thing, to bring men to God, and God to men, so that in His Church and in the world God may have the place He deserves.

"If I be a man of God, let fire come down from heaven," answered Elijah when the captain addressed him. The true God is the God who answers by fire. And the true man of God is he who knows how to call down the fire because he has power with the God of heaven. Whether the fire be that of judgment or the Holy Spirit, the work of the man of God is to bring fire down on earth. What the world needs is the man of God who knows God's power and has power with God.

It is in the secret place of prayer that we learn to know our God and His fire and our power with Him. Oh! To know what is really implied by being a man of God! In Elijah, as in Moses, we see how it means a separation from every other interest, an entire identification with the honor of God, and being no longer a man of the world, but *a man of God.*

Both Moses and Elijah developed into men of

God through being men of prayer and men of the Word. So it is possible, by the same path, for us to become and live as men of God and fulfill the calling God has given us in this world.

7

THE POWER OF GOD'S WORD

"The word of God which worketh in you that believe." (1 Thess. 2:13)

If I know the man who speaks I know whether I can depend on his words or not. If a man promises to give me half of all he has, it makes a big difference whether the speaker is a poor man or a millionaire. One of the first requisites for fruitful Bible study is to know God as the Omnipotent One... and the power of His Word.

The power of God's Word is infinite. "By the word of the Lord were the heavens made. He spake and it was done; He commanded and it stood fast." God's omnipotence works through His Word: it has creative power and calls into existence the very thing of which it speaks.

The Word of the Living God is a living word and gives life. Not only can it call things into existence, but it can even make alive again that which was dead. Its quickening power can raise dead bodies and can give eternal life to dead souls. All spiritual life comes through His Word, for we are born of incorruptible seed by the Word of God that liveth and abideth forever.

Right here, hidden from many, is one of the

deepest secrets of the blessing of God's Word—its creative and quickening energy. *The Word will work in me the very attitude or grace which it commands or promises.* It worketh effectually in them that believe. The power of the Word is irresistible when you receive it into your heart through the Holy Spirit. The voice of the Lord is in power. Everything depends upon learning the art of receiving God's Word into your heart. In learning this art, the first step is *faith in its living, omnipotent, creative power.* It is by His Word that God calleth the things that are not, as though they were.

This was true of all the mighty deeds God did from creation to the resurrection of the dead. It is equally true of every word He spoke to us in His holy book. What keeps us from believing this as we should? The first is that most of the people around us, ourselves included, have such a poor experience with it because of our human wisdom, unbelief, or worldliness. The other reason is because we don't realize the seed aspect of the Scripture. Seeds are small. They may long be dormant. They have to be planted, and even then when they sprout they grow slowly. Because the action of God's Word is hidden and unobserved—its growth slow and apparently weak—we do not believe in its omnipotence. One of the first lessons we must learn is to study the Word as the power of God unto salvation: *it will work in me all that I need, and all that the Father asks.*

This faith would open up wonderful prospects and treasures in our spiritual life. All the blessings of God's grace would be within our reach. God's Word has power to light up our darkness. It will bring the light of God, the sense of His love, and the knowledge of His will directly into our hearts. That same Word can fill us with strength and courage to conquer every enemy and to do whatever God asks of us. The Word would cleanse, sanctify, and work in us faith and obedience. It would become in us the seed of every trait in the likeness of our Lord. Through the Word, the Spirit would lead us into all truth, thus making all that is in the Word true in us. Our hearts would be prepared as the dwelling place of the Father and the Son.

Our morning watch would be transformed in our relation to God's Word if we really believed this simple truth. Let us begin by proving its power in our own experience. Let us quietly set ourselves to exercise the mighty power of God's Word. God Himself will make His Word true in us. We will find out about some things that hinder that power, and we will need to learn how to be freed from these hindrances. We will have to learn more about our own surrender in order to receive that working. But we are on our way if we set out upon our Bible study with the determined resolve to believe that *God's Word has omnipotent power to work every blessing in our heart of which it speaks.*

8

THE SEED IS THE WORD

I believe that in all nature there is no illustration so true and full of meaning of what the Word of God is, as that of the seed. To have full spiritual insight into it is a wonderful means of grace.

The points of resemblance are easy to see: A seed is apparently insignificant—such a little thing as compared with the tree that springs from it. Life is enclosed and dormant within a husk. The seed needs suitable soil or else it cannot grow. Growth is slow, calling for the patience of the farmer. When the fruit inevitably comes, the seed is reproduced and multiplies itself. In all these respects, the seed teaches us precious lessons in our use of God's Word.

The first is *the lesson of faith.* Faith does not look at appearances. It looks most improbable to us that the Word of God could give life to the soul and produce in us the very thing of which it speaks. How could it transform our whole character and fill us with strength? Yet this is true. In believing this we have found one of the chief secrets of our Bible study. From that point on we shall receive each word from God as the pledge and power that He is going to work it in us.

Then there is *the lesson of labor.* The seed must

be gathered and put into the prepared soil. Our minds must gather and understand the words which meet our need from Scripture and then pass them on to the heart. The heart is the only soil in which this heavenly seed can grow. It cannot grow in the mind alone. We cannot give the seed life or growth. We do not have to. Life is intrinsic. Our part is to hide the Word in our heart, keep it there, and wait for the sunshine that comes from above.

The seed teaches *the lesson of patience.* The effect of the Word on the heart is in most cases not immediate. It needs time to sink its roots and start growing. Christ's words must abide in us. Day by day we must increase our store of knowledge from the Word like gathering grain into a barn. More than that, we must watch over those words of command or promise that we have gathered and allow them room in our heart to spread both roots and branches. We need to remember what seed we have put in, and to watch what is going to happen to it with patient expectancy. In due time we shall reap, if we faint not.

And last comes *the lesson of fruitfulness.* The seed of the Word might seem so insignificant. Its life may look so weak, so completely hidden, so slow growing. But *be sure, the fruit will come.* It will grow and ripen within you because it is charged with the power of God. And just as a seed bears a fruit which contains the same seed for new reproduction, so the Word will not only bring you the fruit it promises, but that fruit will each time become another seed which you carry to give life and blessing to others.

Not only the Word, but the kingdom of heaven is also like a seed. Christ is a seed. The Holy Spirit is a seed. The love of God shed abroad in the heart is a seed. The exceeding greatness of the power that worketh in us is a seed. We can be absolutely sure that the hidden life is there, in the heart, but it is not always nor immediately felt in its power. The Divine glory is there, but often not yet recognizable. It has to be known only by faith. We have to count on it and act on it even when we don't feel it. We must wait for its springing forth in growth.

With such a faith attitude, the study of God's Word becomes an act of faith, surrender and dependence upon the living God. My part is to yield my heart hungrily and wholly to receive this Divine seed. Then I wait on God in absolute dependence and confidence to give the increase in power above what I can ask or think.

9

DOING AND KNOWING

"But Jesus said, 'Yea rather, blessed are they that hear the Word of God and keep it.'" (Luke 11:28)
"If any man willeth to do His will, he shall know." (John 7:17)

A young Christian once said to me, "Help me to study my Bible. Give me some rules to guide me; how to begin, and how to go on. I want to know my Bible well." As this is the desire of all sincere Christians, I want to share some thoughts on how we can draw from God's precious Word all that Divine instruction and nourishment, all that abundant joy and strength which God has laid up in it for us.

The thing that comes before all else is the spirit in which you come to Bible study, in the morning watch or at other times. What is your objective or purpose? In worldly matters a person is ruled and urged on by the goal that he sets before himself. It is the same with Bible study. It may surprise you, but if your aim is simply to know the Bible well, you will be disappointed. If you think that thorough knowledge of the Bible will necessarily be a blessing, you are mistaken. To some it is a curse. To others it is powerless: it does not make them either holy or

41

happy. To some it is a burden and it depresses them instead of energizing them or lifting them up.

What then should be the aim, the real attitude of the Bible student? Since God's Word is food—bread from heaven—the first need for Bible study is *a great hunger for righteousness*—a great desire *to do all God's will.* Since the Bible is a light, the first condition for its enjoyment is *a hearty longing to walk in God's ways.* What are we to do with the Word of God? Not just know or hear it, but *keep it.* According to our Lord, all true knowledge of God's Word depends upon there being first *the will to do it.* I want to emphasize this: God will refuse to unlock the real meaning and blessing of His word to any except those *whose will is definitely set upon doing it.* I must read my Bible with the single purpose *to do it.*

This becomes more clear if we realize what *words* are meant for. Words stand between the will and the action. If a man wills to do something for you, before he does it, he expresses his thought or purpose in words. Then he fulfills the words by doing what he promised. It is the same way with God. In creation His word was with power. He spoke and it was done. He does what He says. David prayed, *"Do* as Thou hast *spoken"* (2 Samuel 7:25). Solomon said at the consecration of the temple, "Who hath with His hands *fulfilled* that which He *spake* with His mouth"; "hath performed His Word that He hath *spoken*"; "who *spake* it with Thy mouth, and hast *fulfilled* with Thy hand"; "let Thy word be *verified,* which Thou hast *spoken*" (2 Chron. 6:4,10,15,17). In the prophets God said,

"I the Lord, have *spoken* it; I will *do* it." And they said, "What Thou has *spoken,* is *done.*" The truth and the worth of what God promises consists in just this—that *He does it!* When He gives His word, it is done.

This is also true of His word of command to us, of things which He means *us to do.* We can do many things with God's commands: We can seek to know them; we can admire their beauty; we can praise their wisdom. But if we do not *do them,* we deceive ourselves and fall short of pleasing God. They are meant *to be done.* Only as we do them will their real meaning and blessing be unfolded to us. Only as we do them can we really grow in the Divine life—"walking worthy of the Lord unto all pleasing, bearing fruit unto *every good work"* first, and *then* "increasing in the knowledge of God." We must approach God's words with the same view which God has, *that they should be obeyed.* Only then can we have any hope of blessing from the Bible.

Is not this the same pattern in school, business, career, or any pursuit in life? The pupil or trainee is certainly expected to put into practice the lessons he receives. Only then is he eligible for further teaching. It is the same in the Christian life. Bible study is mere theory, just a pleasing experience or an exercise of mind and imagination, worth little or nothing for a life of true Christlikeness, until the student is determined never to open or close his Bible without making God's purpose His very own. He must be ready to hear and obey when God says, *"Do all* that *I speak."*

This was the mark of great men of God in the past. "So Abram went, as the Lord had spoken to him." "As the Lord had commanded Moses, so did he." Of David we read, "I have found a man after Mine own heart, who shall do all My will." In Psalm 119 we hear him speaking with God about His word, and praying for Divine light and teaching, but always accompanied by his vow of obedience or some other expression of love and delight. Above all, it was the mark of God's own Son, who was single-minded in doing all the will of God.

Dear Christians, I beseech you by the mercies of God, when you ask God to lead you into the treasures of His Word, into the palace where Christ dwells, do it as one who presents himself a living sacrifice. *Be ready to do whatever God speaks to you.* Do not take this for granted. It is of deeper importance than you know. This is more frequently absent from Bible study than you think. Seek for it with deep humility. The prerequisite for enjoying your food is hunger. The first requirement for the study of the Bible is a *simple, determined longing* to find out just what it is God wants you to do, and a dead-in-earnest resolve to do it. "If any man willeth *to do His will,* he shall know of the teaching." To him the Word of God will surely be opened up.

10

THE BLESSEDNESS OF THE DOER

"Be ye doers of the word, and not hearers only, deluding your own selves. But...being not a hearer that forgetteth, but a doer that worketh, this man shall be blessed in his doing." (James 1:22-25)

We greatly deceive ourselves if we enjoy hearing the Word and yet do not put it into action. The sight of multitudes of Christians, regularly and earnestly sitting under the sound preaching of the Bible and doing nothing about it is terribly common. If you hired someone to help you and that person only listened to your instructions and did not carry them out, certainly you would not put up with it. Strangely, many of these Christians do not really know that they are not living good Christian lives. What factors contribute to this self-delusion?

First, people mistake the pleasure of hearing the Word for worship. There is something delightful to the mind to have the truth put clearly before it; the imagination enjoys the illustrations, feelings are stimulated by the applications. Knowledge does give a certain pleasure to an active mind. A person may study some branch of science, for instance, just for the enjoyment that knowledge gives him, without the least intention of applying it practically. In the same way some people go to church and enjoy the preaching and yet *do not do what God asks.* The converted man is not so different from the unconverted if he is content in this.

Another cause of this delusion is the perverted doctrine of our inability to do good. Christians do not really believe that the grace of Christ is able to work obedience in us, to keep us from sinning and to really make us holy. People think that in practice there is no way for them to keep from sinning. "Surely God cannot expect exact obedience from us because He knows we cannot give it." This is an error that strikes at the very root of a determined purpose to do all that God has asked. It closes the heart to any earnest desire to believe and experience all that God's grace can do in us. It keeps us self-centered in the midst of sin. What a terrible delusion to hear and not do!

A third reason that has to do especially with our morning watch and private Bible reading is that hearing or reading is looked upon as a duty, the performance of which is considered to be something religious. We dutifully spend five or ten minutes in the morning reading the Bible; we have read thoughtfully and attentively; we have tried to take in what we read. Well, that ritual faithfully performed eases our conscience and gives us a pleasant sense of satisfaction. But there is scarcely anything that hardens us more to reality than a duty performed or knowledge acquired which has not been applied We have stopped short and accomplished nothing because we have not completed what the Lord desires and expects of us—to go out and do what He said we should do.

It is in the morning watch that this delusion must be fought and conquered. Such attention to doing immediately what God speaks to us may disturb our regular Bible reading schedule. We may even fall behind in it. Although it does not have to be so, if it happens, let it. Far better to fall behind than continue reading without doing. *Everything depends on doing.* It is only that heart which delights in God's law, and has set its will determinedly on doing it, that can receive God's enlightenment. Without this will to do, our knowledge will not profit and will only be head knowledge.

In life, in academic fields and in business, the only way of truly knowing something is to put it into practice. What a person cannot do, he does not thoroughly know. There is just no other way to know God and to taste His blessedness than to do His will. Doing demonstrates whether it is a god of my own emotions or imaginings that I confess, or the true and living God who rules and works all things. There is no possible way under heaven of being united to God other than to be united to His will by doing it. Only by doing His will can I prove that I love and accept it, and make myself one with it. The battleground to have this point settled once for all is right in the quiet of the inner chamber, in the spirit in which I do my private Bible reading. If I determine that *I am going to do whatever God says,* and then put it into action, self-delusion will be overcome.

It may help us if we take some portion of God's

Word and demonstrate how we are to deal with it if
we are determined to do what God says.

For instance, the Sermon on the Mount. I begin
with the first Beatitude: "Blessed are the poor in
spirit." I ask myself, "What does this mean? Am I
obeying this? Am I completely in earnest to try day
by day to maintain this attitude?" When I admit
how far my proud, self-confident nature is from this
ideal, I must be willing to wait before Christ in
surrender and believe that He can work it in me.
"Am I honestly going *to do this*—to try to be poor
in spirit? Or shall I again be a hearer and not a
doer?"

I may go through the Beatitudes and through
the whole Sermon on the Mount in this way, paying
attention to Jesus' teachings on humility and mercy,
on love and righteousness, on doing absolutely
everything as unto the Father, and trusting Him in
all. Verse by verse I will keep asking myself, "Do I
know what this means? Am I living it out? Am I
doing it? Am I the kind of person of whom He
speaks?" We may find ourselves answering "I am
afraid not; I don't see any possibility of living like
that, and doing what He says." At that point I will
feel the need of an entire revision of both my creed
and my conduct. This is a crisis for my determination to do whatever God wants me to do. However,
such questionings may show me that I do have a
considerable degree of these characteristics. Then I
will be led to an entirely new insight into my need of
Christ who will breathe into me His own life and
work in me all that He speaks. I will begin to
develop courage, in faith, to say: "*I can do* all things

through Him who strengtheneth me. Whatsoever He saith in His Word, *I will do.*"

11

KEEPING CHRIST'S COMMANDMENTS

"If ye know these things, blessed are ye if ye do them." (John 13:17)

The subject of doing God's Word is of such supreme importance in the Christian life, and therefore in our Bible study, that I want to return to it once more. Let us explore the one expression, keeping the Word, or keeping the commandments.

Let us look at the repetition of this phrase in the farewell discourse of Jesus:

"If ye love Me, *keep My commandments,* and the Father will send you the Comforter" (John 14:15,16).
"He that *hath My commandments,* and *keepeth them,* he it is that loveth Me, and he shall be loved by My Father" (John 14:21).
"If ye abide in Me, and *My words abide in you,* ask whatsoever ye will, and it shall be done unto you" (John 15:7).
"If ye *keep My commandments,* ye shall abide in My love" (John 15:10).
"Ye are My friends, if ye *do whatsoever I command* you" (John 15:14).

Study and compare these passages until the words enter your heart and work their deep conviction in you. Is not the conclusion that *keeping Christ's commandments is the indispensable condition of all true spiritual blessing?* It is indispensable for the coming of God, the Holy Spirit, into our lives and His actual indwelling. Likewise it is necessary for the enjoyment of the Father's love, the inward manifestation of Christ, and the living of the Father and the Son in the heart. The power of prayer depends on it, as does the abiding in Christ's love and the enjoyment of His friendship. For the power to claim and enjoy these blessings in faith day by day, we need a childlike consciousness that we do keep God's words. It is indispensable for fruitful Bible study that we have the quiet assurance of expecting that every word of God will work in us Divine light and strength because He knows we are ready to obey them completely. The only way to the heart of the Father, and His way to ours, is through delighting in and doing God's will. The way to every blessing is the *keeping of His commandments.*

John's First Epistle confirms all this in a striking way: "Hereby do we know that we know Him, if we *keep His commandments.* He that saith, I know Him, and *keepeth not* His commandments, is a liar. But whoso keepeth His word, in him verily is the love of God perfected" (1 John 2:3-5). Keeping His Word is the only proof of a true, living, saving knowledge of God. It confirms that we have not been self-deceived in our faith; that God's love is not our imagination but an actual possession.

"If our heart condemn us not, we have boldness

toward God; and whatsoever we ask we receive, *because we keep* His commandments. And *he that keepeth* His commandments, abideth in Him" (1 John 3:21,22,24). Keeping the commandments is the secret of confidence toward God and of true intimate fellowship with Him.

"This is the love of God, that *we keep* His commandments, for whatsoever is begotten of God overcometh the world" (1 John 5:3,4). It is no use to profess that 've love unless we prove it by keeping His commandments in the power of the life we receive from God.

When we see the prominence Christ and Scripture give to this truth, we shall learn what prominence we need to give to it in our life. This is one of the keys to true Bible study. A person who reads his Bible with the determined purpose *to search out and obey every commandment of God and of Christ* is on the right track to receiving all the blessings that were ever meant to come from the Word. Such a person will especially learn two things. First, he will see his need to wait for the teaching of the Holy Spirit to lead him into all God's will. Then he will learn what blessedness there really is in performing daily duties, not only because they are right, or he finds enjoyment in them, but simply because they are the will of God. All of daily life will be lifted. The Word will become the light and guide by which all his steps are ordered. Life will become the training school to prove the sanctifying power of the Word. The keeping of His commandments will be the key to every spiritual blessing.

All of this will not come without effort and practice. Take some of Christ's clearest commandments and determine full obedience. Do not allow a sense of failure or lack of power to lead you to despair, or on the other hand, to make you satisfied that you have attained. Let all your efforts to do His will cause you to put your hope more entirely on Him and the working of His Spirit in you both *to will and to do.* Every conviction needs to be carried out into action. There was no other reason that Christ gave His commandments except that they should be obeyed. The mere accumulation of scriptural knowledge only darkens and hardens, and the final result will be some kind of pleasure in the exercise of Bible study which makes us unfit for the Spirit to teach.

Do not become tired of this repetition. We need it most urgently. It is right in our inner chamber that the question is decided whether you will keep the commandments of Christ through the day. Here, too, it will be decided if, in the future, you are to have developed in you the character of a person wholly given up to know and to do the will of God.

12

LIFE AND KNOWLEDGE

"And out of the ground made the Lord God to grow the tree of life in the midst of the garden, and the tree of knowledge of good and evil." (Genesis 2:9)

There are two ways of knowing things. The one is in the mind by an idea or a thought: I know about a thing. The other is in the life: I know by experience. A clever blind person may know all that science can teach him about light, by having books read to him. Nevertheless, a child or an uneducated person, who has never thought about what light is, still knows it far better than the blind student. The blind person knows all about it by thinking; the other knows it in reality by seeing and experiencing it.

It is the same way in faith. The mind can form thoughts about God from the Bible and know all the doctrines of salvation, yet his inner life does not know the saving power of God. This is why we read, "He that loveth not, knoweth not God; for God is love." He may know all about God and about love, even speak beautiful thoughts about it, but unless he expresses love, he does not know God. Only love can know God. That knowledge of God is life eternal.

God's Word is the word of life. Out of the heart are the issues of life. The life may be strong even where knowledge in the mind is weak. You can pursue knowledge very diligently, but your life may still not be affected by it.

I will illustrate this from nature. Suppose we could give understanding to an apple tree, along with eyes to see and hands to work. The apple tree could then do for itself what the gardener now does, gather fertilizer and water itself. But the inner life of the apple tree would be no different, even though understanding had been added to it. It is the same with the inner Divine life of a person. That life is something quite different from the intellect which knows about it. Yes, the function of the intellect is important to offer to the heart the Word of God which the Holy Spirit can then make alive. The intellect is the channel. Yet it is absolutely powerless, either to give or to make the true life alive. It is only a servant who carries the food. It is the heart that must feed and be nourished and live.

The two trees in Paradise are God's revelation of the same truth. If Adam had eaten of the tree of life, he would have received and known all the good that God had for him in living power by experience. He would have known evil only by being absolutely free from it. But Eve was led astray by the desire for knowledge—"the fruit was to be desired to make one wise"—and man got a knowledge of good without possessing it. He got a knowledge of it only from the evil that was its opposite. Since that day man has always sought his religion more in knowledge than in life.

But it is only life, experience, possession of God and His goodness, that gives true knowledge. The knowledge of the intellect cannot make alive. "Though I understand all mysteries and *all knowledge,* and have not love, I am nothing." It is in our morning watch, in our daily Bible reading, that this danger is confronted. Right there it must be met and conquered. Certainly we need the intellect to hear and understand God's Word in its human meaning But we need to know clearly that the possession of the truth by the intellect alone cannot profit. Only the Holy Spirit can make it life and truth in our hearts. So we need to yield our hearts and wait on God in quiet submission and faith so that the Spirit can work it in us. As this becomes our habit, we shall learn how our intellect and heart can work in perfect harmony. Each movement of the mind can always be accompanied by the corresponding movement of the heart, waiting on and listening for the teaching of the Holy Spirit.

13

THE HEART AND THE UNDERSTANDING

"Trust in the Lord with all thine heart, and lean not unto thine own understanding."
(Proverbs 3:5)

The chief objective of the Book of Proverbs is to teach knowledge and discernment, and to guide us in the path of wisdom and understanding. It also offers a warning about pursuing this by cautioning us to distinguish between trusting our own understanding and intellect, and seeking spiritual understanding. The latter is that which God gives—an understanding heart. We always have the two powers within us, the intellect and the heart. Either one of them can be applied to our seeking after knowledge and wisdom, in all our everyday plans, or studying the Word.

I am deeply persuaded that one of the main reasons for so much Bible study, Bible teaching, and Bible knowledge being comparatively fruitless is because we trust to our own understanding. That holds equally true for the lack of holiness, love and power in the Church.

Many will argue that since it is God, after all, who gave us our intellect, there is no other way of knowing God's Word. While this is true, there is also another aspect. Our whole human nature was disordered when man fell. The will became enslaved, the emotions were perverted, and the understanding was darkened. Most people admit the ruin resulting from the fall in the first two areas, but deny it in practice in the latter. They admit that even the believer does not have within him the power of a holy will and so needs the daily renewing of the grace of Jesus Christ. They admit that he does not have the power of holy emotions to love God and his neighbor without the Holy Spirit working in him all the time. But they fail to notice that the intellect is just as much spiritually ruined and incapable of grasping spiritual truth. Was it not especially the desire for knowledge, in a way and at a time that God had forbidden it, that led Eve astray? Our greatest danger is still to think that we can take the knowledge of God's truth out of His Word by ourselves. We need to be deeply convinced of the powerlessness of our understanding to really know His truth and become aware of the terrible danger that self-confidence and self-deception present. We need to see why the counsel "Trust in the Lord with all thine heart, and lean not to thine own understanding" is so much needed.

It is with the heart man believes. It is with all the heart that we are to seek, and serve, and love God. It is only with the heart that we can know God or worship Him, in spirit and in truth. The Word of God clearly declares all those things. It is in the heart, therefore, that the Divine Word does the work. It is into our hearts that God sent the Spirit of His Son, not into our minds. What is the heart? The inward life of desire and love and will and surrender. That is where the Holy Spirit guides into all truth. We must be careful to apply this in our Bible study.

We should not trust the understanding that comes from our natural selves. The only thing it can give us is thoughts and ideas of Divine things without reality. It will deceive us into thinking that if we just receive the truth into our minds, it will automatically enter the heart. We will be so blinded with that idea that God will not be able to get through to us. It is a terrible universal experience that people read God's Word daily and every Sunday they delight to hear God's Word, but the result is that they are made neither humble, nor holy, nor heavenly-minded by it.

How shall we overcome then? Instead of trusting the understanding, we should come to the Bible with the heart, trusting in the Lord. Let us set our whole heart upon the living God as the Teacher when we begin our morning watch. Then God will give us an understanding heart, a spiritual understanding.

You may ask, as I have often asked myself, "Tell me in a practical way how I should study my Bible to avoid relying upon my own understanding. I don't see any way of not doing it."

You are partly right. You cannot bypass your understanding. But do not use it for what it cannot do. Remember two things. One, that the understanding that comes from yourself can only give you a picture or idea of spiritual things. Accept that, but right away go with your heart to the Lord, asking

Him to make His Word life and truth in you. The other is that the pride of your intellect and the danger of leaning on your own understanding will always be with you. Nothing, not even your most determined purpose, can save you from this permanently. The secret is the continual dependence of your heart on the Holy Spirit's teaching. Only the Holy Spirit can make God's Word alive in your heart, in your attitude and emotions, and guide your intellect. "The meek will He guide in judgment; the meek will He teach His way." "The fear of the Lord," an attitude, "is the beginning of wisdom."

Whenever your understanding grasps a thought from the Word, bow immediately before God in dependence and trust. Believe with your whole heart that God can and will make it true.. Ask for the Holy Spirit to work it out effectively in your heart and life. In that way the Word becomes the strength of your life.

If you persevere in this, the time will come when the Holy Spirit, dwelling in your heart and life, will begin to hold your understanding in control and let God's holy light shine through it.

14

GOD'S THOUGHTS AND OUR THOUGHTS

"As the heavens are higher than the earth, so are My thoughts higher than your thoughts." (Isaiah 55:9)

When a wise person says something, his words often have a different or deeper meaning from what the hearer understands. How much more do the words of God, as He understands them, mean something infinitely higher than we can casually understand.

Why should we especially need to remember this? Because it will continually keep us from being satisfied with our knowledge and thoughts about the Word. We will wonder and wait for the full blessing of them as God meant them. It will give a new urgency to pray for the Holy Spirit to teach us and show us what has not even occurred to our hearts to receive. We will have confidence to hope that there is, even in this life, a fulfillment beyond our highest thoughts.

Therefore God's Word has two meanings. The one is that which it has in the mind of God. The other is our weak, partial, defective apprehension of it. The human words are actually the bearers of all the glory of God's Divine wisdom, power and love.

By grace and experience we may think that words like the love of God, the grace of God, and the power of God are very true and real to us. But there is still an infinite fullness in the Word that we have not even touched.

Who would dream of trying to reach the sun or the stars with his short arm? To climb the highest mountain wouldn't help either. This is an illustration of God's truth that His thoughts are higher than our thoughts. Even when the Word has expressed God's thoughts as accurately as our minds can take them in, it is still a fact that they are higher than our thoughts as the heavens are higher than the earth. All the infinities of God and the eternal world are contained in the Word like a seed. As the full-grown oak is so mysteriously greater than the small acorn from which it sprang, so God's words are the seeds from which God's mighty wonders of grace and power grow.

Faith in His Word should teach us two lessons: the one is how little we know; the other is how much we should expect. We are to come to the Word as little children. Jesus said, "Thou hast hid these things from the wise and prudent, and hast revealed them unto babes." The wise spoken of are not necessarily hypocrites or enemies. They can be God's own dear children as well. By neglecting to cultivate a childlike spirit, they have spiritual truth hidden from them and never become spiritual men. Such persons would rather depend on the scripturalness of their creed, or the diligence of their Bible study for their growth. "Who among men knoweth the things of a man, save the spirit of the man, which is in him?

Even so the things of God none knoweth, save the Spirit of God. But we received the Spirit of God, that we might know." Our Bible study should be characterized by a deep sense of how ignorant we are, and how much we should distrust our own power to understand the things of God.

The more we realize our inability to grasp the thoughts of God, the greater will be our expectancy that He wants to make His Word true in us. The Holy Spirit is already in us to reveal the things of God. As we pray in true humility and faith, God will give us an ever-growing insight into the mystery of God through the Holy Spirit's enlightenment. What is that mystery of God? Our wonderful union and likeness to Christ, His living in us, and our being as He was in this world.

Also, God will answer our prayers even more fully. If our hearts thirst and wait for it, the time may come when, by a special communication of His Spirit, all our expectations will be satisfied and Christ will take possession of our hearts so that what was faith for so long, becomes our experience.

15

MEDITATION

"Blessed is the man whose delight is in the law of the Lord, and in His law doth he meditate day and night." (Psalm 1:1,2)
"Let the words of my mouth and the meditation of my heart be acceptable in Thy sight, O Lord." (Ps. 19:14)

The true aim of education, study and reading is not in what we take in, but what is expressed from ourselves. Information received should awaken our inward power which in turn should be actively exercised. This is as true of the study of the Bible as of any other study. God's Word only works its true blessing when the truth it brings to us has stirred the inner life and then has reproduced itself in resolve, trust, love and worship. When this happens, the Word is productive; it has done what God sent it to do. It has become part of our life and strengthened us for new purpose and action.

Meditation is the medium through which this takes place. In the thought process the understanding takes in the meaning and implications of a certain fact. So in meditation, the heart takes in and absorbs a thought to make it a part of its own life. We need to continually remind ourselves that when we speak of the heart, we mean the will and the emotions. The meditation of the heart implies desire, acceptance, surrender, and love. Out of the heart are the issues of life. What the heart truly believes, it receives with love and joy, and allows to master and rule the life. The intellect gathers and prepares the food on which we are to feed. In meditation, the heart takes it and eats it.

The art of meditation does not come automatically; we have to develop it. Meditation is mentioned seven times in Psalm 119. Each time it is part of a prayer addressed to God. "I will meditate in *Thy precepts.*" "Thy servant did meditate in *Thy statutes.*" "O how I love *Thy law,* it is my meditation all the day." Meditation is the heart turning toward God with His Word and trying to absorb it into the emotions and will—our very life. Just as a person is trained to concentrate his mental powers to think clearly and accurately, a Christian needs to cultivate meditation. This power of meditation is developed by, first, presenting ourselves before God; we must know His presence. Second, we must form the habit of yielding our hearts wholly to God and His Word. His Word has no power of blessing apart from Him. His Word is meant to bring us into His presence and fellowship. Practice His presence and take the Word as directly from Him, and be assured He will make it work in your heart.

When we study Scripture and try to grasp an argument, or master a difficulty, our mind needs to put forth great effort. The attitude of meditation is different. True meditation is quiet restfulness. It is a process of letting the truth settle in and become part of us, not by striving but through a peaceful process. We plant or hide the truth in our hearts and let it germinate quietly. From our Lord's mother we have the example: "Mary kept all these things and pondered them in her heart." In her attitude we have the pattern of a person who has begun to know Christ and wishes to stay on the sure way to know Him better. That is meditation.

In meditation the personal application takes first place. This does not always happen with the intellectual study of the Bible, the object of which is to know and understand. By contrast, in meditation the chief object is to appropriate and experience. A readiness to believe every promise implicitly, to obey every command unhesitatingly, to "stand perfect and complete in all the will of God," is the only true spirit of Bible study.

Meditation must lead to prayer. It provides material for prayer. It must lead us to ask God and to receive definitely what it has seen in the Word. The value of meditation is that it prepares us to pray for what the Word has revealed that we need or that is possible for us. That is where the rest of faith comes in, that looking upward with the assurance that the Word will be proven in us in power when we surrender to it.

In the course of time, the result of resting in meditation, after intellectual effort, will be that the two, meditation and intellect will be brought into harmony in understanding God's Word. All of our Bible study will be made alive by the spirit of quiet waiting on God and a yielding of our heart and life to the Word.

Our fellowship with God is meant to last the whole day. If we secure the presence of God through meditation in our morning watch, we will be brought closer to the experience of the man in the first Psalm: "Blessed is the man whose delight is in the law of the Lord, and in His law doth he *meditate day and night.*"

Workers and leaders of God's people need meditation even more than others, if they are to train others, and also keep up their own unbroken communication with the only Source of strength and blessing. God says, "I will be with thee; I will not fail nor forsake thee. Only be thou strong and very courageous that thou mayest *observe to do* according to all the law...that thou mayest prosper whithersoever thou goest. This book of the law shall not depart out of thy mouth; *thou shalt meditate therein day and night...* .Then thou shalt have good success... . Be strong and of good courage."

"Let the words of my mouth and the meditation of my heart, be acceptable in Thy sight, O Lord, my Strength and my Redeemer." Let it be your highest aim that your meditation may be acceptable *in His sight.* Let that be part of the spiritual sacrifice you offer God. Let your prayer and expectation be first of all that your meditation may be true worship, the living surrender of your heart to God's Word in His presence.

16

REVEALED UNTO BABES

"I thank Thee, Father, Lord of heaven and earth, that Thou hast hid these things from the wise and prudent, and revealed them unto babes." (Matt. 11:25; Luke 10:21)

The wise and prudent are persons who are conscious of the powers of their own minds and count on their reason to help them understand Divine knowledge. Babes are those who do not depend on their own minds, but upon the heart. Ignorance, helplessness, dependence, meekness, teachableness, trust and love—such are the attitudes God seeks in those who He wants to teach (Ps. 25:9, 12, 17, 20).

One of the most important parts of our devotions is the study of God's Word. So the most important thing we can do is to approach the Word in the spirit of waiting for God to reveal His truth to us. It is indispensable to have a childlike, even babe-like attitude. To such the Father loves to impart the secrets of His love. With the wise and prudent, head knowledge comes first; from them God hides the spiritual meaning of *the very thing they think they understand.* With babes it is just the opposite; the heart and the feeling, the sense of humility, love and trust, is first. To them God reveals, in their inner life and experience, *the very thing they know they cannot understand.*

In education there are two styles of teaching. The ordinary teacher makes the communication of knowledge his chief object, and tries to develop the abilities of the child to attain his object. The better teacher considers the amount of knowledge a secondary thing. His first aim is to develop the power of the mind and spirit and to help the pupil, both mentally and morally, to use his abilities correctly to acquire and apply knowledge.

There are also two kinds of preachers. Some pour out instruction and argument and appeal continuously and just leave it to those who hear to make the best use of it. The more effective preacher realizes how much depends upon the state of the heart and tries, even as our Lord Jesus did, to subordinate the teaching of objective truth or doctrine to the cultivation of those attitudes which profit most. Wise and prudent Christians can listen to a hundred eloquent and earnest sermons thinking they can understand and profit from them by their own reason. But one sermon heard by Christians who have a childlike consciousness of their spiritual poverty and are open and ready to obey will result in receiving much more of the Father's teaching.

In the secret chamber, every person is on his own as far as human help is concerned. He must train himself in the habit of approaching God with babe-like simplicity and teachableness. It was not only necessary that God revealed His truth to the world, but that He continues to reveal it to each individual by the Holy Spirit. That is what we must wait for in our inner life. In this position we exercise the babe-like spirit and receive the kingdom of God as a little child.

All evangelical Christians believe in regeneration. But how few believe that when a man is born of God, *a babe-like dependence on God for all teaching and strength ought to be his chief characteristic.* It was the one thing our Lord insisted on above all. He declared that the poor in heart, the meek, the hungry, were blessed. He called men to learn of Him because He was meek and lowly in heart. He spoke of our humbling ourselves and becoming as little children. Why? Because the first and chief mark of being a child of God, of being like Jesus Christ, is *an absolute dependence upon God for every blessing, and especially for any real knowledge of spiritual things.*

Let each person ask himself: Have I considered the babe-like attitude the first essential in my study of the Bible? Of what use is my Bible study without such an approach? It is the only real key to God's school. Would it not be wise to set aside everything else to secure this? Only then will God reveal His hidden wisdom.

By the new birth, when we become God's children, we are made babes. The childlike spirit is meant to persist in us even as we move to maturity. It remains the requirement to receive God's revelation. The first thing a wise workman does is to see that he has the proper tools and that they are in good working order. It is not lost time for him to stop his work and sharpen his tools. For us, it is not lost time to let our Bible study wait until we are sure we are in the right attitude of a babe-like receptiveness. If you conclude that you have not been reading your Bible in such a spirit, confess and forsake at once your self-confident spirit of being like the wise and prudent. Not only pray for it, but believe for it. It is in you by the new birth, though you may have neglected and suppressed it. You may begin at once as a child of God to experience it.

Do not try to bring about this spirit in your heart by reflection or argument. Work outward from within. It is in you, as a seed, in the new life, born of the Spirit. It must rise and grow in you. Then you can exercise it by living as a babe before God. As a new-born babe, desire the milk of the Word. Let this attitude permeate your permanent mind-set and the state of your heart all the day, not just when you study Scripture. Only then can you enjoy the continual guidance of the Holy Spirit.

17

LEARNING OF CHRIST

*"Take My yoke upon you and learn of Me,
for I am meek and lowly of heart, and ye
shall find rest to your souls."* (Matt: 11:29)

All Bible study is learning. All Bible study
should be learning of Christ if it is to be fruitful. The
Bible is the school book and Christ is the Teacher. It
is He who opens the understanding, opens the heart,
and opens the seals (Luke 24:45; Acts 16:14; Rev.
5:9).

Christ is the living, eternal Word, of which the
written words are the human expression. Christ's
presence and teaching are the secret of all true Bible
study. The written Word is powerless unless it helps
us into the presence of the Living Word. No one can
say that our Lord did not honor the Old Testament.
He affirmed that He loved it as coming directly
from the mouth of God. He always pointed the
Jews to it as the revelation of God and the witness
to Himself. But notice that when He spoke with His
disciples how frequently He spoke of His own
teaching as being what they needed most and had to
obey. Only after His resurrection, when they were
one with Him by having received the first breathings
of the Holy Spirit (John 20:22), was He able to open

their understanding of the Scriptures. The Jews had their own reasoned interpretation of the Word, and they made it the greatest barrier between themselves and Jesus, although it spoke of Him. It is often the same with Christians. Our human apprehension of Scriptures, fortified as it may be by the authority of the Church or our own circle, becomes the greatest hindrance in receiving Christ's teachings. Christ the Living Word wants to be our only Teacher. Only if He is, shall we learn of Him to honor and understand Scripture.

Learn of Me, for I am meek and lowly of heart. In this statement our Lord opens to us the inmost secret of His own inner life. That was what fitted Him to be a Teacher and a Saviour. That is what He wants to give to us and what He wants us to learn of Him. This is the one virtue that makes Him the Lamb of God, our suffering Redeemer, our heavenly Teacher and Leader. If we have this attitude, all else will issue from it. This is the one condition we should apply not only to our Bible study but to our whole Christian life. He, the Teacher, meek and lowly of heart, wants to make you what He is. As a learner you must come and study His disposition and seek to learn from Him how you can have it too.

Why is this so all-important? Because it is at the root of the true relationship of the creature to the Creator. Only God has life and goodness and happiness. As the God of love He delights to give and work everything in us. Christ became the Son of Man in order to show us the kind of unceasing dependence upon God we should have. That is the meaning of His being lowly in heart. In this spirit the angels veil their faces and cast their crowns before God. God is everything to them and they delight to receive all from Him and to give all to Him.

What is the root of the true Christian life? To be nothing before God and men; to wait on God alone; to delight in, to imitate, to learn of Christ, the meek and lowly one. This is the only key to the true knowledge of Scripture. It is in this attitude that Christ comes to teach and only in this attitude that you can learn of Him. What an insignificant place the Church has given to the teaching of humility compared to its significance in the life of Christ and the teachings of God's Word. I am deeply persuaded that this is the reason for much of the weakness and unfruitfulness in the Church. Only when we are meek and lowly in heart can Christ teach us by His Spirit what God has for us and what God will work in us.

Let each of us start with himself to value this as the first condition of discipleship. We will find it to be the first lesson the Master most surely teaches us. Let us approach our Bible study this way. In due time our morning watch will be the scene of daily fellowship and blessing.

I have great difficulties myself in making this the first consideration of my Bible study. But it is essential. In communion with God, attitude and character are everything. It is hard to make people realize that a meek and lowly heart is the very seed and root and without it, there is very little profit in Bible study. It is even harder to convince believers that we can have this attitude because a meek and lowly heart is the very thing Christ offers to give. He teaches us to find and receive it directly in Himself.

No matter how difficult this discipline is, I urge all Bible students to thoughtfully and prayerfully ask themselves whether the very first question to be settled in the inner chamber is not this: Is my *heart* in the state in which my Teacher wants it to be? And if it is not, the first thing I must do is to yield myself to Him to work it in me.

18

TEACHABLENESS

*"Take my yoke upon you and learn of Me,
for I am meek and lowly of heart; and ye
shall find rest to your souls."* (Matt. 11:29)

The first characteristic of a good student is
receptiveness and a willingness to be taught. What
does this imply? That there is something you do not
know, and that you are ready to give up your own
thinking or doing and look at things from the
teacher's viewpoint. You have a quiet confidence
that the teacher knows and will show you how to
learn and to know. The meek and lowly spirit listens
carefully to know what the teacher's will is, and
immediately hurries to carry it out. If a student has
such an attitude, it must be the teacher's fault if he
does not learn.

How does it happen that, with Christ as our
Teacher, there are so many failures and so little real
growth in spiritual knowledge? So much hearing
and reading of the Bible, so much profession of
faith in it as our only rule of life, and yet such a lack
of expression of its spirit and power? So much time
actually spent in private devotions and in Bible
study groups but with so little evidence of the joy
and strength that God's Word is meant to give?

These are very important questions. There must be some reason why so many disciples of Jesus think they honestly want to know and do His will, but by their own admission, and confirmed by those around them, are so powerless in witness to others. If we could find the answer, there would be a lot of changed lives.

The Bible verse at the beginning of this chapter suggests the answer: many have taken Christ as a Saviour *but not as a Teacher.* They have put their trust in Him as the Good Shepherd who gave His life for the sheep; but they know little of the reality of His daily shepherding, or of hearing His voice when He calls them by name, or following only Him. They know little of what it is to follow the Lamb; to receive from Him, above all, the lamb's nature; and to seek, like Him, to be meek and lowly in heart. It was by their three year course in His school that Christ's disciples were fitted for the baptism of the Holy Spirit, and the fulfillment of all the wonderful promises He had given them. It is under the personal teaching of our Lord Jesus, and through that gentleness of the meek and lowly heart, which daily waits for and receives and follows that teaching, that we can truly find rest to our souls. All that weariness and burden of strain and failure and disappointment then gives way to that Divine peace which knows that all is being cared for by Christ Himself.

The attitude of our whole life, every day and all day, is to take Christ's yoke and learn His disposition. In so doing we shall become teachable and refuse to act in our own wisdom. It is especially in the morning hour that this is to be cultivated. There we should first seek deliverance from self and all its energy. While occupied there with the words of God and of Christ and of the Holy Spirit, we will realize that the only profit in them is when Christ teaches us personally through them. Unless Jesus Himself comes near and takes charge of us in the inner chamber, we cannot receive His teaching. Again, teachableness is everything. If it is true that the Holy Spirit "shall teach you all things" it is equally true that the whole attitude of our life must be a receptivity to His teaching. Only in this way can our daily interaction with God's Word be what the Lord Jesus wants to make of it.

Unlearning is often the most important part of learning: wrong impressions and prejudices are obstacles to learning. Until these have been removed, the teacher labors in vain because he communicates knowledge only to the surface. Deep underneath the student is still guided by that which has become second nature to him. The teacher must first lead the student to discover and remove those hindrances himself.

Unless we are willing to unlearn, we can't learn of Christ fruitfully. Our hindrances to God's truth come from heredity, education, tradition, and our own thoughts about religion and the Bible. To learn of Christ means that we are really willing to subject every truth we hold to His inspection for criticism and correction.

Humility is the root virtue of the Christian life. "He that humbleth himself shall be exalted" is one of God's absolutes. Our disappointment in not attaining higher degrees of spiritual life is caused by lacking this lowliness. "God giveth grace to the humble" has a far wider and deeper application than we think.

Our readiness to be taught is one form of humility. In the morning watch we present ourselves as learners in Christ's school. Let teachableness and humility be our distinguishing marks as learners. And if we feel we fall short, let us listen to the voice that says, "Take My yoke upon you...learn of Me, for I am meek and lowly of heart...and ye shall find rest to your souls."

19

THE LIFE AND THE LIGHT

"In the beginning was the Word. And the Word was God. In Him was life, and the life was the Light of men." (John 1:1,4)
"He that followeth Me shall not walk in darkness, but shall have the light of life." (John 8:12)

Because Christ was God, He could be the Word of God. Because He had the life of God in Himself, He could be the revealer of that Life. Therefore, as the Living Word He is the Life-giving Word. The written Word can count for nothing if human wisdom is trusted for its understanding. Only when we accept the written Word as a seed in which the Living Word lies hidden, can it be made alive by the Holy Spirit and become to us the Word of life. Our contact with God's written Word should always be related to our faith in the Eternal Word, who was God.

The same truth comes out in the next expression: The life is the light. When we see light shining, we know that there is fire burning in some form. It is so in both the natural and spiritual world. There must be life before there can be light. There may be reflected light or borrowed light without life, but only true life can show true light. He who follows Christ is promised to have the light of life.

These two statements of one great truth strikingly confirm what we have learned about the Spirit of God. In the same way that the Spirit knows the things of God because He is the life of God, so Christ is the Word because He is God and has the life of God. Therefore the light of God only shines where the life of God is. All three thoughts apply to our approach to Bible study. Only through the Holy Spirit can God's Word be made life and truth within us and enable us to receive a blessing from it.

So we come back to the one great lesson that the Spirit is reinforcing as we relate to God's Word: Only as Scripture is received out of the life of God into our life, can there be any real knowledge of it. Where it is received as a seed in the good soil of our hungry heart, it will grow up and bring forth fruit, like all seed, "after its kind." It will reproduce in our life the very life of God out of which it came. In us will grow the same likeness and characteristics of the Father and the Son through the Holy Spirit. Let us become very practical and apply it directly to our private Bible study.

Do you want to know how to begin? The rules are very simple.

First, "Be still and know that I am God." Take time to become quiet and recognize God's presence. "Hold thy peace at the presence of the Lord." "Be silent before the Lord." "The Lord is in His Holy temple; let all the earth keep silence before Him." Worship and wait on God so that He may speak to you.

Next, remember that the Word comes out of the living heart of God and is carrying His life into your heart. Only the power of God can make it live in you.

Next, set your faith in Christ the Living Word, as the Life and the Light that He said He was, and that He promised us. Follow Jesus in love and longing desire, in obedience and service. When you do that, His life will work in you and His life will be the light of your soul.

After that, ask the Father for the Holy Spirit, who is the only one who knows the things of God, to make the Word in your heart living and active. Hunger for the will of God as you do for your daily food. Thirst for the living spring of the Spirit within you. Receive the Word into your will, your life, your joy.

The reason I have emphasized this truth in the last few chapters is very simple. My own experience has taught me how long it takes before we clearly understand that the Word of God has to be received into the life and not only into the mind, and how long after the Word is understood before we fully believe it and act upon it. To write the same thing to you is not grievous to me, and for you it is profitable. Study the lesson until you know it.

You may be surprised to find that this lesson takes more time to learn than you think, simple as it is. Do not be afraid and do not be impatient. Be sure that if you learn it correctly, you will be so thankful to God that it has become a key that you never had before. You will unlock the hidden treasure of the Word and find true wisdom in the hidden part.

So I repeat again the simple words that are so inexhaustibly blessed and true: Only the Spirit of God knows the things of God. So only when the Spirit of God lives in me can He make me know the things of God by imparting them to my life. Only as I receive the life of Christ through the Word do I have the light of the knowledge of God.

20

THE BIBLE STUDENT

"Blessed is the man whose delight is in the law of the Lord; and in His law doth he meditate day and night." (Psalm 1:1,2)

All around us we hear the loud call for more, and for truer Bible study. Evangelists like D.L. Moody and many others have proved what power there is in preaching directly from God's Word, inspired by faith in its power. Earnest Christians have asked: "Why can't our ministers speak the same way and give the Word of God a larger place in their ministry?" Many young ministers have come out of seminary confessing that they have been taught everything else except the knowledge of how to study the Word by themselves, and then how to stimulate and help others to study it. In some of our churches, the desire has been expressed that this lack in the training of ministers has to be remedied. It might appear to be very simple to find good men to undertake that work and yet it has been found very difficult. It seems that men with theological training do not find it easy to be simple and direct in their approach to God's Word so that they can show the younger men how to make Scripture the one source of their knowledge and teaching. In the student movement of our day, thank God, Bible study is having the place of prominence that it should have. God's Word must have its true place in the work to be done for Him. Let us look at the principles behind the demand for more Bible study and how we can do something about it.

1. God's Word is the only authentic revelation of God's will. All human statements of Divine truth, however correct, are defective and carry a measure of human authority. In the Word of God, the voice of God speaks to us directly. Every child of God is called to direct communion with the Father through the Word. As God reveals all His heart and grace in the Word, His child can, if he receives it from God, get all the life and power in that Word into his own heart and life. We are aware how few secondhand reports of messages or events can be fully trusted. Very few men can report accurately what they have heard. Every believer has the right and the privilege to communicate directly with God. God has revealed Himself in His Word and He continues to do so to every believer.

2. This Word of God is a living Word. It carries a Divine quickening power in it. The human expression of the truth is often a mere conception or image of the truth. It appeals to the mind and has little or no effect. It gets its power only when we have faith that it is God's own Word. Everything needs form in order to be known or expressed. The words in which God has chosen to clothe His own Divine thoughts are God-breathed. The life of God dwells in them. God is not the God of the dead but of the living. The Word was not only inspired when first

given: the Spirit of God still breathes in it. God is still in and with His Word. Christians and teachers need to believe this. They must have the simple confidence that the Word of God is different from all human teaching.

3. God Himself alone can, and most surely will, be the Interpreter of His own Word. Divine truth needs a Divine Teacher. Spiritual apprehension of spiritual things can only come from the Holy Spirit. When we are deeply convinced that God's Word is unique, above all other words of men, we will urgently feel the need for supernatural, directly Divine teaching. Then we are on the way to knowing wisdom in the hidden parts which are in the heart and attitude. Light and life will come as a result.

4. The Word then brings us into the closest and most intimate fellowship with God—unity of will and life. God has revealed His whole heart and all His will in the Word; in His law and precepts He tells us what to do; in His redemption and His promises He tells us what He will do for us. As we accept that will and yield ourselves to let it work out through us, we will learn to know God in His working power. This should be our highest aim and experience in all our Bible study.

Let us now apply these four thoughts in a practical way.

In the Holy Scripture we have the very words in which the Holy God has spoken and in which He speaks to us today.

These words are, today, full of the life of God God is in them and He makes His presence and power known to believers who seek Him in them. To those who ask and wait for the teaching of the Holy Spirit, the Spirit will surely reveal the spiritual meaning and power of the Word.

Therefore the Word is meant to be the daily means of God revealing Himself to you and His way of having fellowship with you.

Have we learned to apply these truths? Do we understand that the Word always calls us? Seek God. Listen to God. Wait for God. God will surely speak to you. Let God teach you. All we hear about more Bible teaching and more Bible study must lead to this one thing. We must be examples of people who know that the Word is never separated from the Living God Himself. *We should live as those to whom God in heaven speaks every day and all day long.*

21

WHO ART THOU?

"Set your mind on the things that are above...for ye died and your life is hid with Christ in God." (Col. 3:2,3)

As you enter God's presence in the morning hour, much depends upon your realizing not only who God is, but who you, yourself, are. You need to know where you stand in relation to God. If we claim right of access and an audience from the Most High, we need to be ready to answer the question, "Who art thou?" We need to know our place in Christ before God.

Who am I? Yes, let me think about it and express who I am that I should ask God to meet me here and spend the whole day with me. I know; by the Word and the Spirit of God, that I am in Christ, and that my life is hid with Christ in God. In Christ I died to sin and the world. I am now taken out of them, separated from them and delivered from their power. I have been raised together with Christ and in Him I live unto God. So I come to God to claim and obtain all Divine life that is hidden in Him for the supply and need of my life today.

Yes, this is who I am. I say it to God in humble, holy reverence. I say it to myself to encourage others, as well as myself. I am one who longs to say that Christ is my life. The longing of my soul is for Christ, revealed by the Father Himself within my heart. Christ is the only one who can satisfy me. My life is hid .with Christ. The only way He can be my life is to be in my heart. Yes! That is the only way I can be content. Christ is my Saviour from sin. Christ is the gift and bearer of God's love. Christ is my indwelling Friend and Lord.

Oh, my God! If You ask me, "Who art thou?" listen to my stammering: I live in Christ and Christ lives in me. You alone can make me understand all that this means.

I come desiring and seeking to be prepared to express the life of Christ today on earth, to translate His hidden heavenly glory into the language of my daily life, with its attitudes and responsibilities. As Christ lived on earth only to do the will of God, it is my great desire to stand perfect and complete in all His will. My ignorance of that will and how to apply it spiritually in my contacts with the world and people is very great. My incapability is even greater. And yet I dare approach God without seeking any compromise, but in all honesty I accept the high calling to live fully the will of God in all things.

This is what brings me to the inner chamber to meet God. As I think of all my failures in fulfilling God's will, as I know that there will be temptations and dangers awaiting me, as I feel my entire insufficiency, I still say to God—I am coming. Yes, I am coming to claim the life hid in Christ, so that I may live my life for Christ. I feel drawn on in the assurance that God will go with me and bless me.

Who am I that I should ask these great and wonderful things of God?

Should I really expect to live the life hid with Christ in God so that it can be expressed in my mortal body? I may. God, Himself, will work it in me by the Holy Spirit dwelling in me. The same God who raised Christ from the dead, and then set Him at the right hand, has raised me with Him and given me the Spirit of the glory of His Son in my heart. God is going to work in me and maintain increasingly in me a life in Christ by the Holy Spirit. When I come in the morning and present myself before Him to take up afresh the life He has hidden in Himself, I can wait for the Father to give me the fresh anointing that teaches all things. I can expect Him to take charge of the new day He has given me.

My brother, my sister, I am sure you feel how infinitely important it is to take a firm stand on God's presence when you come to Him in the morning hour...and believe what He says to you. Accept what God has given you in Christ. Be consciously and openly what God has made you to be. Take time before God to know it and to say it. In a battle, much depends upon your unwavering position. Take your place *where God has placed you.*

Again, the very attempt to do this may at times interfere with your ordinary Bible study or prayer. Never mind, it will not be a loss. It will be fully compensated for later. Your whole life depends upon knowing who your God is, and *who you are as His redeemed one in Christ.* Your everyday life depends on it. When once you have learned the secret, you will not even have to be conscious of it.

It will be the strength of your heart, both in going in to God, and going out with Him to the world.

Brenda Memorial Library
The Salvation Army
School for Officers' Training
Suffern, N.Y.

22

THE WILL OF GOD

"Thy will be done on earth as it is in heaven." (Matt. 6:10)

The will of God is the living power to which the world owes its existence. Through that will, and according to that will, it is what it is. The world is the expression, manifestation, and embodiment of God's will in its wisdom, power, and goodness. The beauty and glory of the world exists only because God willed it. God's will formed the world and upholds it every day. Creation is doing what it was destined to do, for it shows forth the glory of God. "They gave glory to Him that liveth for ever and ever, saying, 'Thou art worthy to receive glory, for Thou hast created all things, and because of Thy will they are, and were created.' "

This is true of both inanimate nature and intelligent creatures. Divine will created a creature with a will, man, in His own image and likeness. Man has the living power to know and accept and co-operate with that Will to which he owes his being. Unfallen angels count it their highest honor and happiness to be able to will and do exactly what God wills and does. The glory of heaven is that God's will is done there. The sin and misery of fallen angels and men consists in their having turned away from, and refusing to abide in and to do, the will of God.

Redemption is simply the restoration of God's will to its place in the world. For this reason Christ came into the world and demonstrated in human life how man has only one thing to live for—the doing of God's will. He showed us how there was one way to conquer self-will—by a death to it, in obeying God's will even unto death. He atoned for our self-will and conquered it for us, opening a path through death and resurrection into life devoted to the will of God.

God's redeeming will is now able to do in fallen man what His creating will did in nature, or in unfallen beings. Christ gave us the example of what God expects of us in devotion to and delighting in His will. In Christ and His Spirit He renews and takes possession of our will. He works in it both to will and to do all His will.

He is doing the work in us. "He makes us perfect in every good thing to do His will, working in us that which is pleasing in His sight." As this is revealed by the Holy Spirit, and believed, and received into the heart, we begin to get an insight into the prayer, "Thy will be done on earth as it is in heaven." Our desire is awakened for that very thing.

It is essential that the believer realize his relation to God's will and its claim on him.

Many, many believers have no idea of what their faith or their feeling should be in relation to the will of God. Few people say, "My whole motivation is to be in complete harmony with the will of God; I don't want to do anything other than God's will for me. By God's grace I want every hour of my life to be lived in the will of God, doing it as it is done in heaven."

When faith in God's will masters our heart, then we shall have the courage to believe in the answer to the prayer our Lord taught us. We must understand that only by close union with Christ can all this happen in us. Then we will realize that we, too, can do our part, that our weak will on earth can correspond to the will of God. When it is our destiny, our obligation, and our heart's desire that God's will may be done in us and by us as it is in heaven, then our faith will overcome the world.

Our will cannot be disconnected from the fact of our living union with the Father nor the living presence of His Son. Only by Divine guidance given through the Holy Spirit can the will of God truly be known in its beauty, in its application to daily life, and its ever-growing revelation. Again, it will only be given to those with childlike attitudes, who are willing to wait for and depend on what is given them.

Our secret communion with God is the place where we repeat and learn these great lessons. The God whom I worship asks me to unite perfectly with His will. My worship means: "I delight to do Thy will, O God." It is in the morning hour, in the inner chamber, that I can learn God's will and surrender myself joyfully to do all His will. Then my study of God's Word and my prayer will bear fruit in full blessing.

23

FEEDING ON THE WORD

*"Thy words were found and I did eat them;
and Thy word was unto me the joy and
rejoicing of my heart."* (Jer. 15:16)

In this verse you have three actions: The *finding*
of God's Word, which only comes to those who
seek diligently for it. Then the *eating,* which means
the personal appropriation of the words of God for
our own needs. "Man shall not live by bread alone,
but by every word that proceedeth out of the mouth
of God." And then the *rejoicing,* "The Kingdom of
Heaven is like unto treasure hid in a field which,
when a man hath found, he hideth, and for the joy
thereof goeth and selleth all that he hath, and
buyeth that field." In the foregoing verse, too, we
have the finding, the appropriating, and the
rejoicing.

The central thought here is eating. It is preceded
by the searching and the finding. It is accompanied
and followed by rejoicing. That which is aimed for
is used, and there is a result. Much depends upon
eating God's words in the inner chamber.

There is a great difference between the finding
and the eating. It can be illustrated by comparing
the corn a farmer has stored up in his barn, with the

bread he has on his table. Sowing, cultivating, har-
vesting his grain is essential, but cannot profit him
until he eats the bread in daily portions as his body
requires. In the finding stage, great quantity and
speed of work are important. Eating is the
opposite—a small quantity, at regular intervals,
appropriated slowly, is the need.

Do you see how this applies to your Scripture
study in the morning watch? You need *to find* God's
words, master them by careful thought, store them
in your mind and memory for your own use and
that of others. Certainly there is joy in this, too: joy
of harvest or of victory, the joy of treasure secured,
or difficulties overcome. Yet we must remember
that this finding and possessing the words of God is
not that eating of them which is the only thing
bringing Divine life and strength to us.

Just because you possess it, good wholesome
corn will not nourish you. The fact that you are
deeply interested in the knowledge of God's Word
will not of itself nourish your soul. The thing that
brings rejoicing is that you actually eat them.

And what is this eating? In eating you so completely assimilate the corn that it becomes part of
yourself, entering into your blood, forming your
very flesh and bone. This has to be done in a small
quantity at a time, two or three times a day, every
day of the year. This is the law of nourishment. It is
not the amount of truth that I gather from God's
Word that is important. It is not how interested I
am or how successful in studying my Bible. It is not
how clearly I see God's truth or how much I grasp
at a time that results in the health and growth of my

spiritual life. Not at all. All this may still leave my nature very much unsanctified and unspiritual, with very little of the holiness or humility of Jesus. Something else is needed. Jesus said that His meat was to do the will of Him that sent Him. That implies taking a small portion of God's Word, some definite command or duty of the new life in Christ; quietly receiving it into the will and the heart; yielding the whole being to its rule; deciding, in the power of Jesus, to perform it; and then doing it. This is what it means to eat the Word, to take it into our inmost being in such a way that it becomes a constituent part of our very life. A truth or a promise should be handled the same way. What you eat becomes such a part of yourself that you carry it with you wherever you go.

Do you see now how this illustration covers all your Bible study? Scriptural knowledge is one thing, assimilating it is another. You can gather and store grain to last for years, but you cannot swallow a large enough quantity of bread to last for days. Day by day, and more than once a day, you eat your food. So the eating of God's Word must be in small portions, just as much as your soul can receive and digest at one time. This must go on from year to year.

George Muller said he learned that he should not stop reading the Word until he felt happy in God: then he felt fit to go out to his day's work. That is finding, eating, and rejoicing in God's work in perfect illustration.

24

HOLIDAYS

*"If the master of the house had known in
what hour the thief was coming, he would
have watched and not left his house to be
broken through."* (Luke 12:39)

A prominent educator declared, "It is very
important what you do with your leisure hours since
this affects your character the most. Leisure hours
are the hinge on which true education turns."

It is true that character comes first in importance and after that the training of skill and
strength. A teacher can do only so much to stimulate and to guide, but every student has to work out
his own character. How true it is that in the leisure
hours, when free from constraint and observation, a
person shows what is really most important to him.

In our Christian faith this is intensely true.
Thousands of students have felt it, without knowing
how to express or explain it. At college or school
their morning watch was much easier to put into
their schedule. The mind of a student is geared to
regular and systematic work, and the Christian student keeps his time for devotions as strictly as he
does for his class or study period.

But when the time for relaxation comes, when

one is free to do exactly as one likes, many find that the morning watch and the fellowship with God does not come as naturally as they thought. It is not looked upon as such a necessity of the spiritual life, and such a joy, that it should continue during our holiday pleasure. The holiday becomes the test of character, the proof of how far one could say with Job, "I have esteemed the words of Thy mouth more than my necessary food." Do you see how the question of leisure hours is all important? In them I turn freely and naturally to whatever I love most. In leisure I prove and increase the power to hold what I have.

A teacher in a large school is reported to have said, "The greatest difficulty with which we have to contend is the summer vacation. Just when we have brought a student up to a good point of discipline, and he is responding to the best ideals, we lose him. When he comes back in the autumn, we have to begin all over again. The summer holiday simply demoralizes him." This statement, as it refers to ordinary study and responsibility, is strong. But within certain limits, it is no less applicable to the Christian life. The sudden relaxation of regular habits, and the subtle thought that one has perfect freedom to do as one likes and what brings perfect happiness, throws many a young student back in his Christian life. It is certainly necessary that older and more experienced members of the students' groups should help and guard their younger members in this area. The attainment of months may be lost by the neglect of a week. We do not know in what hour the thief comes. The spirit of the morning watch means that we must have unceasing vigilance all day and every day.

The student may avoid some of these dangers if he is aware of them. Holidays mean freedom from school disciplines. But there are disciplines of morality and of health from which there is no relaxation. The student must realize that the call to daily fellowship with God belongs not to the former but to the latter class. Just as he needs to eat and breathe every day during the holidays, he needs to eat the bread and breathe the air of heaven every day.

Decide within yourself that the morning watch is not only a duty, but an unspeakable privilege and pleasure. To the new spiritual nature, fellowship with God, abiding in Christ, loving the Word and meditating on it all the day are life and strength, health and gladness. Look upon them in this light. Believe in the power of the new nature within and act upon it. Though you do not feel it, it will become real. As you count it a joy, it will become a joy to you.

Above all, realize that the world needs you and depends on you to be its light. Christ is waiting for you as a member of His Body, day by day, to do His saving work through you. Neither He, nor the world, nor you, can afford to lose a single day. Why has God created and redeemed you? So that through you, as through the sun He lightens the world unceasingly every day, His light and life and love can shine out upon men. You need new communication with the Fountain of all light every day. Don't think of asking for a holiday from such communion with the Divine. And don't *take* it. Look upon the holiday as a special time of extra study beyond your ordinary habit. Prize your holiday for the special opportunity of more fellowship with the Father and the Son. Instead of holidays becoming occasions for sliding back and exhausting your energies in just keeping up, look upon them as blessed times for grace and victory over self and the world. You will reap a great increase of grace and strength, of being blessed and being made a blessing.

25

THE INWARD AND THE OUTWARD

"Ye fools, did not He that made that which is without make that which is within also?"
(Luke 11:40)

The outward form or shape is the visible expression of the hidden inward life. We are generally aware of the outward before the inward. Through it the inward is developed and reaches its full perfection, as the Apostle says in 1 Corinthians 15:46: "Howbeit that is not first which is spiritual, but, which is natural; then that which is spiritual." One of the greatest secrets of the Christian life is to understand and maintain the right relation between the inward and the outward.

If Adam had not listened to the tempter, his trial would have resulted in the perfecting of his inward life. Instead it became his sin and ruin, and the cause of all his misery. Why? Because he gave himself up to the power of the visible outward world. He did not seek his happiness in the hidden inward life of a heart in which God's command was honored, in the inward attitudes of love and faith, of obedience and dependence. He fixed his desire on the world outside of himself, on the pleasure and the knowledge of good and evil that he thought it could give him.

All false religion, from the most degrading idolatry to corrupted forms of Judaism and Christianity, has its root in emphasis on the outward. What can please the eye, interest the mind, or gratify the taste, takes the place of that truth in the inward part, that hidden wisdom in the heart and life which God seeks and gives.

The great mark of the New Testament is that it is a dispensation of the inner life. The promise of the new covenant is: "I will put My law *in their inward parts* and *in their hearts* will I write it." "A new heart also will I give you and a new spirit will I put *within you,* and I will put My Spirit *within you."* The promise of our Lord Jesus was "The Spirit of truth *shall be in you.* In that day ye shall know that *I am in you."* Our faith consists in the state of heart, in a heart into which God has sent forth the Spirit of His Son, a heart in which the love of God is shed abroad. There is found true salvation. The inner chamber, with its secret fellowship with the Father, who sees in secret, is the symbol and the training school of the inner life. The faithful daily use of the inner chamber will make the inner hidden life strong and happy.

In our Christian life the great danger is that we give more time and interest to the outward means than the inward reality. It is not the intensity of your Bible study, nor how often you do it, or how fervent are your prayers or good works, that necessarily make up a spiritual life. No! We need to realize that, as God is a Spirit, so there is a spirit within us that can know and receive Him and become conformed to His likeness and be a partaker of His image.

Settle this in your mind, that your salvation consists in expressing the nature, life and spirit of Christ Jesus in your outward and inward new man. Wherever you go, whatever you do, while at home or in outside affairs, do all in a desire to retain union with Christ, reflecting His attitudes and will. Put priority on those things which exercise and increase the spirit and life of Christ in your soul, and that contribute toward changing you into the likeness of the holy Jesus.

Consider the treasure you have within you—the Saviour of the world, the eternal Word of God, hid in your heart as a seed of the Divine Nature. That Nature is to overcome sin and death within you and generate the life of heaven again in your soul. Turn to your heart, and your heart will find its Saviour, its God, living there. The reason some people see and feel nothing of God is because they seek for Him outside, in books, in the church, in its outward exercises. They will never find Him there. He is found first in the heart. Seek for Him in your heart and you will never seek in vain. That is where He dwells; that is the seat of His light and Holy Spirit!

26

THE DAILY RENEWAL—ITS POWER

*"Though our outward man perish, yet the
inward man is renewed day by day."*
(2 Cor. 4:16)
*"According to His mercy He saved us, by
the washing of regeneration, and renewing
of the Holy Ghost."* (Titus 3:5)

Nature renews its life every day. As the sun rises
again with its light and warmth, the flower opens,
and the birds sing, life is everywhere stirred and
strengthened. As we rise from resting in sleep and sit
down for our breakfast, we feel that we have
gathered new strength for the duties of the day.

By meeting God in the inner chamber we confess that our inward life also needs daily renewal. It
is only by fresh nourishment from God's Word, and
fresh communion with God Himself in prayer, that
the vigor of our spiritual life can be maintained and
grow. Though our outward man perish, though we
are burdened with sickness or suffering, though the
strain of work and weariness may exhaust or make
us weak, the inward man can be renewed day by
day.

A quiet time and place, with the Word and
prayer, are the means of that renewal. But these can

only be effective as a means when they are animated by the Divine power which works through them. That power is the Holy Spirit, the mighty power of God who works in us. Our study of the inner chamber and the inner life which it represents would be incomplete if we did not emphasize the daily renewal of the inward man, which is the special function of the Spirit. In the verse from Titus we are taught that we have been "saved by the *washing of regeneration* and *renewing of the Holy Ghost.*" The two expressions are not meant to be a repetition. The regeneration is the one great act, the beginning of the Christian life; the renewing of the Holy Ghost is a work that is carried on continuously and never ends. In Romans 12:2 we read of the progressive transformation of the Christian life, that it is by *"the renewing of the mind."* In Ephesians 4: 22,23, the verb in the phrase "put off the old man" is in the aorist tense and indicates an act done once for all. The verb in *"be renewed in the spirit of your mind"* is in the present tense and points to a progressive work. Even so in Colossians 3:10 we read, "Ye have put on the new man, which *is* renewed (not has been renewed) in the image of Him that created him." We are to look to the Holy Spirit, on whom we can count for the daily renewal of the inner man in the inner chamber.

In our secret devotions, everything depends on our maintaining our relationship to the adorable Third Person of the Trinity, through whom alone the Father and the Son can do their work of saving love, and through whom alone the Christian can do his work. The relation may be expressed in the two very simple words, *faith* and *surrender.*

Faith: Scripture says, "God hath sent forth the Spirit of His Son into your hearts crying, 'Abba, Father.' " Even the weakest child of God who wants to offer up prayer in his morning watch that will be pleasing to God, must remember that he needs to depend on the Holy Spirit as indispensable for doing that. If the daily renewal of the inward man in the morning hour is to be a reality, we have to take time to meditate, and to worship, and to believe with our whole heart that the Holy Spirit is within us to work through prayer and the Word.

Surrender: Do not forget that the Holy Spirit must have entire control. "As many as are *led by the Spirit* of God, they are the sons of God" (Rom. 8:14). "They *walk after the Spirit,* not after the flesh" (Rom. 8:4). It is the ungrieved presence of the Spirit that can give the Word its light and power, and keep us in a spirit of childlike confidence and obedience that pleases God. Let us praise God for this wonderful gift, the Holy Spirit in His renewing power, and let us look with new joy and hope to the inner chamber. That is the place provided by God where our inner man can be renewed from day to day. So shall life be kept ever fresh; so shall we go on from strength to strength and bear much fruit, that the Father may be glorified.

If all this is true, what a need there is that we should know the Holy Spirit in the right way. As the Third Person of the Trinity, it is His ministry to bring the life of God into us, to hide Himself in the depth of our being, and make Himself one with us. There He reveals the Father and the Son to be the mighty Power of God working in us, and takes control of our entire being. He asks only one thing—simple obedience to His leading. The truly yielded soul will find the secret of growth and strength and joy in the *daily renewing of the Holy Ghost.*

27

THE DAILY RENEWAL—THE PATTERN

*"Seeing that ye have...put on the new man,
which is being renewed unto knowledge
after the image of Him that created him."*
(Col. 3:9,10)
*"If so be that ye heard Him and were taught
in Him...that ye be renewed in the spirit of
your mind, and put on the new man, which
after God hath been created in righteousness and holiness of truth."* (Eph. 4:21,23,24)

In everything you attempt to do, you must have
a clearly defined goal. It is not enough to have
movement and progress, it has to be in the right
direction, straight for the mark. Especially when we
are acting in partnership with someone else on
whom we are dependent, do we need to know that
our aim and his are in perfect accord. If our daily
renewal is to be effective and attain its object, we
need to know clearly what our purpose is.

"Ye have put on the new man, which is being
renewed unto knowledge." The Divine life, the work
of the Holy Spirit within us, is no blind force of
nature. We are to be workers together with God;
our cooperation is to be intelligent and voluntary,
".. unto knowledge." There is a kind of knowledge

which the natural understanding can draw from the Word, but which is without the life, the power, the real truth and substance, which spiritual knowledge brings. It is the renewing of the Holy Ghost that gives true knowledge. That does not consist of thought or idea, but is an inward tasting, a living receiving of the very things of which the words and thoughts are images. No matter how diligently we may study the Bible, we get no further in gaining spiritual knowledge than we have experienced through spiritual renewal. Only as we are renewed in the spirit of our mind, in our inward being, do we obtain true Divine knowledge.

What is the pattern that will be revealed out of this renewal within us? The new man is being renewed unto knowledge, *after the image of Him that created him.* It is the image and likeness of God. That is the aim that the Holy Spirit has in renewing us daily, and it should be our aim as we seek that renewing.

God's purpose in creation was, "Let us make man in Our image, after Our likeness." Consider how glorious these words are. The actual reason God breathed His own life into man was to reproduce in man, on earth, a perfect likeness to God in heaven. In Christ we saw that image of God in human form. We have been predestined, redeemed, called, and are being taught and fitted by the Holy Spirit, to be conformed to the image of the Son. We are to be imitators of God, to walk even as Christ walked. Our daily prayer and Bible study is pointless unless we set our heart on what God has set His: *renewing us in His own image.*

In the second passage we have the same thought expressed somewhat differently. The likeness of God that we are to be renewed into has to do with righteousness and holiness. Righteousness is God's hatred of sin and maintenance of the right. Holiness is God's glory in the perfect harmony of His righteousness and love, His being exalted above man whom He created, yet being perfectly united with him. Righteousness in man includes doing all that God wills for us in our duty to Him and to our fellowmen. Holiness is our personal relationship to Himself. As the new man has been created, so it has to be daily renewed. That is what the Holy Spirit is working in us to accomplish. It happens as we yield ourselves to Him day by day in the morning hour.

How greatly we need meditation and prayer to get the heart set upon what God is aiming at, and get a true vision that it is an actual possibility. Christian student! Do not let anything else be your aim or satisfy you. As you approach Him, expect to find Him, and trust that He is working His likeness in you by the renewing of the Holy Spirit. Let it be your daily prayer to be renewed after the image of Him who created you.

28

THE DAILY RENEWAL—ITS COST

"Wherefore we faint not; but though our outward man is decaying, yet our inward man is renewed day by day." (2 Cor. 4:16) *"Be not fashioned according to this world; but be ye transformed by the renewing of your mind."* (Rom. 12:2)

It is not an easy thing to be a full-grown, strong Christian. On God's side, it means that it cost the Son of God His life. More than that, it needs the mighty power of God to create a new man, and the unceasing daily care of the Holy Spirit to maintain that life.

From man's side it demands that when the new man is put on, the old man must be put off. We are to put away all the dispositions, habits and pleasures of our own nature, that make up the life in which we have lived. We have to sell all that we received by our birth from Adam if we want to possess the pearl of great price. If a man wants to come after Christ, he must deny himself, and take up his cross—forsake all to follow Christ in the path in which He walked. Not only is he to put away sin, but also everything that may be considered needed, legitimate, and precious which may potentially become the occasion of sin. Scripture tells us to pluck out the eye, or cut off the hand, if that becomes a problem leading us to sin. He is to hate his own life and to lose it, if he is to live in "the power of an endless life." It is a far more serious thing than most people think, to be a true Christian.

This is especially true of the daily renewing of the inward man. Paul speaks of it as being accompanied and conditioned by the decaying of the outward man. The whole epistle of 2 Corinthians shows us how the fellowship of the sufferings of Christ, even to conformity to His death, was the secret of Paul's own life in power and blessing to the churches. "Always bearing about in the body the dying of Jesus, that the life also of Jesus may be manifested in our body. For we which live are always delivered unto death for Jesus' sake, that the life also of Jesus may be manifested in our mortal flesh. So then death worketh in us, but life in you." If we want to fully experience the life of Christ within us, in our body, and in our work for others, it will depend upon our fellowship in His suffering and death. There can be no large measure of the renewal of the inward man without the sacrifice and decaying of the outward.

To be filled with heaven, life must be emptied of earth. We have the same truth in our second text, "Be ye transformed by the renewing of your mind." An old house may be renewed and still keep very much of its old appearance. On the other hand, the renewal may be so entire that people exclaim about the transformation. The renewing of the mind by the Holy Spirit means an *entire transformation;* a completely different way of thinking, judging, deciding. The fleshly mind is replaced by a "spiritual understanding" (*cf* Col. 1:9; 1 John 5:20). The cost of this transformation is to give up all that is of the natural. "Be not fashioned according to this world." By nature we are of this world. When we are renewed by grace, we are still in the world, subject to the subtle all-pervading influence from which we cannot get away. What is more, the world is still in us, as the leaven of the natural. Nothing can purge this except the mighty power of the Holy Spirit filling us with the life of heaven.

These truths must take deep hold of us and master us. We cannot go any faster in this daily renewing than the speed with which we free ourselves of being in conformity with the world. Both the positive and the negative need to be emphasized. The spirit of this world and the Spirit of God are battling for the possession of our being. Only when we renounce and cast out the former can the heavenly Spirit enter in and do His renewing and transforming work. But it will cost us the whole world and whatever is of the worldly spirit. It will look very costly as long as we are hesitating about it, or trying to do it in our own strength. But after we really learn that the Holy Spirit does it all, and have given up all to Him, the renewing becomes the simple, natural, healthy, joyous growth of the heavenly life in us.

Then the inner chamber becomes the place where we long to go every day to praise God for what He has done, is doing, and what we know He will do. Day by day it will be delightful to yield ourselves afresh to the Lord who said, "He that believeth on Me, out of him shall flow rivers of living water." "The renewing of the Holy Ghost" becomes one of the most blessed truths of our daily Christian life.

29

HOLINESS—THE CHIEF AIM OF BIBLE STUDY

"Sanctify them in Thy truth; Thy Word is truth." (John 17:17)

Receiving the words of God from Christ, and keeping them, is the mark and power of true discipleship.

Christ prayed that the Father would keep His disciples in the world after He had left it. They could only be kept if they were sanctified in the truth, as they dwelt and worked in His Word. If they kept these words, that would really enable them to live the life and do the work of true disciples. Christ said of Himself, "I am the truth." He was the only begotten of the Father, full of grace and truth. His teaching was not like that of the law which came by Moses and promised things to come. That kind of truth was just an image or a shadow. "The words I speak unto you are spirit and life," giving the very substance and power and Divine possession about which they spoke. Christ had spoken of the Spirit as the Spirit of truth, who would lead them into all the truth that there was in Himself. This was not a matter of knowledge of doctrine, but was to lead into the actual experience of truth. Then He prayed that this living truth, as it dwelt in the Word and was revealed by the Spirit, would be used by the Father to sanctify them. "For their sakes," He said, "I sanctify Myself that they themselves may also be sanctified in truth." He asked the Father to take charge of them by His power and love so that His object of sanctifying them might be realized. Let us study the wonderful lessons that this implies.

The great object of God's Word is to make us holy. We will not have any profit from our Bible study, no matter how diligent or successful we are, unless it makes us more humble and holy. This must definitely be our main object in all our use of the Scriptures. The reason that so much Bible reading has so little result in Christlike character is that salvation through sanctification of the Spirit and belief in the truth is not truly sought. People imagine that if they study the Word and accept its truths, some way this will, of itself, benefit them. But experience teaches that it does not. We only get what we seek. Christ gave us God's Word to make us holy. When the definite aim of all our Bible study is to know the Word in its Divine quickening power, not just doctrinal truth, it will open to us.

It is God Himself who alone can make us holy by His word. The Word, separate from God and His direct operation, cannot profit. The Word is an instrument which God Himself must use. God is the only one who is holy, so only He can make us holy. God's Word is the means of holiness. The serious mistake that many people make is that they forget that only God can use the Word or make it profitable. I do not gain anything by just having access to a dispensary where there are medicines. I need the doctor to prescribe what I need. Without the doctor my use of his medicines may be fatal. That was the problem with the scribes who boasted in God's law. They delighted in their study of Scripture but remained unsanctified. The Word did not sanctify them because they did not seek for this in the Word, and did not yield themselves to God to do it for them.

This holiness through the Word must be sought and waited for from God in prayer. Our Lord prayed to the Father that He would sanctify His disciples. We need to know God's Word and meditate on it. We need to set our heart on being holy as our priority in studying the Word. But all that is not enough. Everything depends upon our following Christ's example in asking the Father to sanctify us through the Word. *It is God, the Holy Father, who makes us holy* by the Spirit of holiness who dwells in us. He works in us the very mind and attitude of Christ who is our sanctification. "There is none holy but the Lord"; all holiness is His and what He gives by His holy Presence. The tabernacle and the temple were not holy because they were cleansed or separated or consecrated. They became holy when the Lord God came in and dwelt there and took possession of them. So God makes us holy through His Word bringing Christ and the Holy Spirit into us. The Father cannot do this unless we wait before Him quietly, in deep dependence and full surrender. As we pray for it, we will find God's sanctifying power. Then our knowledge of God's Word will truly make us holy.

How sacred is the morning watch! It is the hour

especially devoted to our yielding ourselves to God's holiness, to be sanctified through the Word. Let us always remember that the one aim of God's Word is to make us holy. Let it be our continual prayer, "Father, sanctify me in Thy truth."

30

PSALM 119 AND ITS TEACHING

"Oh how I love Thy law; it is my meditation all the day. Consider how I love Thy precepts. Yea, I love them exceedingly."

In Holy Scripture there is one portion entirely devoted to teaching us the place which God's Word ought to have in our life, and the way we can secure its blessing. It is the longest chapter in the Bible, and with hardly an exception, in every one of its 176 verses the Word is mentioned under different terms. Anyone who really wants to know how to study the Bible according to God's will ought to make a careful study of this psalm. Each of us ought to resolve to study its teaching and carry it out in practice. No wonder our Bible study does not bring more spiritual profit and strength if we have neglected the Divine directory it offers us for that study. Is it possible that you have never read it through once as a whole? If you do not have time, find time. Read it straight through and try to take in its main thoughts, or at least catch its spirit. If you cannot do this by reading it once, read it more than once. That will make you feel the need of giving it more careful thought. The following hints may help you in its study:

1. Note all the different names referring to God's Word.

2. Note all the different verbs expressing what we ought to feel and do with regard to the Word. Then consider carefully what place God's Word has in your own heart and life. Is every faculty of your being—desire, love, joy, trust, obedience, action—affected by the Word?

3. Count and note how many times the writer speaks in the past tense of his having kept, observed, stuck to, delighted in God's testimonies. How many times he expresses in the present tense how he rejoices in, loves, and esteems God's law. And then how, in the future tense, he promises and vows to observe God's precepts to the end. Put all these together and see how more than a hundred times he presents his soul before God as one who honors and keeps His law. Study especially how these expressions are connected with his prayers to God, until you have a clear image of the righteous man whose fervent, effectual prayer availeth much.

4. Go on to study the prayers themselves and note down the different requests he makes with regard to the Word. Is he praying to be taught to understand, to have the power to obey it, or for the blessing promised in the Word and to be found in doing it? Note especially prayers like, "Teach me Thy statutes," "Give me understanding." Also those where the plea is "according to Thy Word."

5. Count the verses in which there is any allusion to affliction, whether from his own situation or from his enemies, or the sins of the wicked, or of God delaying "to help him." Learn how we need

God's Word in a special way in the time of trouble, and how this alone can bring comfort to us.

6. Then comes one of the most important things. Note how often the little pronoun Thou, Thine, Thee, occurs, and how often it is understood in petitions like "Teach (Thou) me," "Quicken (Thou) me." You will soon see how the whole psalm is a prayer spoken to God. Everything is spoken upward into the face of God. The psalmist believes that it is pleasing to God and good for his own soul, to connect his meditation and thoughts on the Word as closely as possible with the living God. Every thought of God's Word, instead of drawing him away from God, leads him to fellowship with God.

The Word of God becomes the rich and inexhaustible material for him to hold communion with the God whose it is and to whom it is meant to lead. As we gradually get an insight into these truths we get a new meaning from the single verses. When we take a whole paragraph with its eight verses, we shall find how they help to lift us up, with and through the Word, into God's presence. We enter into that life of obedience and joy which says, "I have sworn, and will perform it, that I will keep Thy righteous judgment." "Oh how I love Thy law; it is my meditation all the day."

Let us seek by the grace of the Holy Spirit to have the kind of devotional life which this psalm reveals. *Let God's Word* every day, and before everything else, *lead us to God.* Let everything in God's Word be turned into prayer, especially our need of Divine teaching. Let us say in a childlike attitude, "Father, help me." Then let us follow our prayers with the resolve that as God quickens and blesses us, we shall run the way of His commandments. Let all that we gain from God's Word make us more eager to carry that Word to others, whether for the awakening or the strengthening of their spiritual lives.

31

THE HOLY TRINITY

"For this cause I bow my knees to the Father,...that He would grant you...that ye may be strengthened with power through His Spirit in the inward man; that Christ may dwell in your hearts through faith, to the end that ye, being rooted and grounded in love, may be strong...to know the love of Christ which passeth knowledge, that ye may be filled unto all the fullness of God. Now unto Him that is able to do exceeding abundantly above all that we ask or think, according to the power [the Holy Spirit], that worketh in us, unto Him be the glory in Christ Jesus for ever and ever. Amen."
(Eph. 3:14-21)

There is good reason for these words being regarded as one of the highest expressions of the believers' life on earth. Yet there is a built-in danger that we should view this as an exceptional and distant experience. The truth is it is meant to be the certain and immediate heritage of every Christian.

Each morning every believer has the right and need to say: "My Father will strengthen me today with power. He is strengthening me even now, in the inner man through His Spirit." Each day we should be satisfied with nothing less than recognizing Christ dwelling in us by faith and that the work of being filled with all the fullness of God is in process within us. Each day we should be so strong in the faith of God's power that we should expect to be able to do above what we ask and think, according to the power of the Spirit working in us.

This passage is remarkable for the way it presents the truth of the Trinity's bearing on our practical life. We need to give special attention to the three Persons of the Trinity at different times as we pursue the Christian life. Some Christians find it difficult to combine the truths of the Trinity and to know how to worship the Three in One. This passage reveals the wonderful relationship and action of the Trinity in perfect unity. We have the Spirit within us as the power of God, and yet He does not work at our wish or on His own. It is the Father who, according to the riches of His glory, grants us to be strengthened "through the Spirit in the inner man." It is the Father who does exceedingly abundantly above what we ask or think "according to the power that worketh in us." The Spirit does not detract us from the Father, but makes us more absolutely and unceasingly dependent on the Father. The Spirit can only work as the Father works through Him. We need to combine the two truths—a deep, reverent, trustful consciousness of the indwelling Holy Spirit and a continual, dependent waiting on the Father to work through Him.

Even so with Christ. We worship God as Father in the name of the Son. We ask Him to strengthen us through the Spirit so that Christ may dwell in our heart. So the Son leads to the Father and the Father again reveals the Son in us. As the Son dwells in the heart, and it is rooted and grounded in love, the heart draws its life out of the soil of Divine love and brings forth fruits by doing the works of love. We are then led on to be filled with all the fullness of God and the whole heart with the inner and outer life becomes the scene of the blessed interchange of the operation of the Trinity. As our hearts believe this, we give glory through Christ to Him who is able to do more than we can think by His Holy Spirit.

This is what our Christian life is meant to be every day. Oh! let us worship the Triune God in the fullness of faith every day. No matter what direction our Bible study and prayer will take, let this always be the center from which we go out and to which we return. We were created in the image of the Trinity. Let us worship and wait; let us believe and give Him glory.

Have you ever noticed in Ephesians how the three Persons of the Trinity are always mentioned together:

The Father, Jesus Christ, spiritual [or Holy Ghost] blessings. (Eph. 1:3)

The Father, to the praise of His glory, in Christ, sealed with the Holy Spirit. (Eph. 1:12,13)

The Father, our Lord Jesus, the Spirit of wisdom. (Eph. 1:17)

Access through Christ, in one Spirit, to the Father. (Eph. 2:18)

In Christ, a habitation of God, through the Spirit. (Eph. 2:22)

The mystery of Christ, hid in God, preached by the grace of God, revealed by the Spirit. (Eph. 3:4-9)

One Spirit, one Lord, one God and Father. (Eph. 4:4-6)

Filled with the Spirit, giving thanks to God, in the name of Christ. (Eph. 5:18-20)

Strong in the Lord, the whole armor of God, the sword of the Spirit, praying in the Spirit. (Eph. 6:10-18)

As you study and compare these passages, and try to gather their teaching in some true and humble conception of the glory of God, notice especially what an intensely practical truth this is of the Holy Trinity. Scripture teaches little of its mystery in the Divine nature. Almost all it has to say refers to God's work in us, and our faith and experience of His salvation.

A true faith in the Trinity will make us strong, bright, God-possessed Christians. The Divine Spirit makes Himself one with our life and inner being; the blessed *Son* dwells in us, as the way to perfect fellowship with God; the *Father,* through the *Spirit* and the *Son,* works His purpose out in us day by day. That is what it means to be filled with all the fullness of God.

Let us bow our knees before the Father! Then the mystery of the Trinity will be known and experienced.

32

IN CHRIST

"Abide in Me, and I in you." (John 15:4)

All instruction proceeds from the outward to the inward.

When we learn some facts, in words or deeds, in nature or history, our mind looks for the meaning hidden in them. It is the same with the teaching of Scripture concerning Jesus Christ. He is presented to us as a man among us, before us, above us, doing a work for us here on earth, and continuing it in heaven. Many Christians stop at this concept of Jesus as an external, exalted Lord in whom they trust for what He has done and is doing for them and in them. They know and enjoy very little of the power of the true mystery of Christ in us, of His inward presence as an indwelling Saviour.

The first three Gospels present the first and simpler view. The Gospel of John represents the latter. The Scriptural doctrine of justification comes from the former but the union of the believer with Christ and His continual abiding is taught in the Gospel of John and in the Epistles to the Ephesians and Colossians.

All Christians who are reading this book should be preparing to carry Christ to their fellowmen. I want to say very earnestly to you: Be sure that this abiding in Christ and Christ in you is not only a truth of doctrine that you hold, but that it also animates all your faith in Christ and communion with God as a matter of life and experience. To be in a room means to have all that there is in it at your disposal—its furniture, its comforts, its light, its air, its shelter. To be in Christ, to abide in Christ, oh! do you know what that means? It must not be a matter of intellectual faith or idea, but a spiritual reality.

Think who and what Christ is. Consider Him in the five aspects or stages that reveal His nature and work. He is *the Incarnate One,* in whom we see how God's Omnipotence united the Divine and human nature perfectly. Living *in Him* we are partaking of the Divine nature and of eternal life. He is *the Obedient One,* living a life of entire surrender to God and perfect dependence on Him. Living *in Him* our life becomes completely surrendered to God's will and we continually wait upon His guidance. He is *the Crucified One,* who died for sin so that He might take it away. Living *in Him* we are free from sin's curse and control, and we live, like Him, in death to the world and our own will. He is *the Risen One,* who lives forevermore. Living *in Him* we share His resurrection power, and walk in newness of life—a life that has triumphed over sin and death. He is *the Exalted One,* sitting on the throne and carrying on His work for the salvation of men. Living *in Him* His love possesses us, and we yield ourselves to Him so that He may use us in winning the world back to God. Being in Christ, abiding in Him, means above all that God has placed us in this wonderful environment of the life of Christ, human and Divine at the same time, and in that position we are wholly filled with God in resurrection life and glory. The elements in which we live, the air we breathe, the environment in which our life exists and grows, are part of the nature and character of Christ Himself. That is *abiding in Christ*.

The indwelling of Christ is the secret of this full manifestation. Because Christ is Divine and all powerful, He can, just so far as we abide in Him, dwell in us. He is limited by the extent to which we surrender to Him and actively obey Him. We can say it because we know it: *Christ liveth in me*.

The main point I wish to make is that if this kind of abiding life is to be our real working-day life, its spirit must be renewed and strengthened by the personal communion with God as we begin each day in the morning watch. If you feel that you want to get nearer to God, to realize more of His presence, power, love, will, or to work more fully for Him, then come to God *in Christ*. Consider how Jesus, as a man on earth, approached His Father in deep humility and dependence, in full surrender and entire obedience. Then you come to the Father in the same spirit, in union with Him. In Christ we can come to God as Christ did. We can count confidently on our approach being accepted, not according to our attainment, but by the completeness of our acceptance in Christ.

33

HIMSELF ALONE

"When Jesus therefore perceived that they would come and take Him by force to make Him a king, He departed again into a mountain Himself alone." (John 6:15)

The Gospels frequently tell us of Christ's going into solitude for prayer. Luke mentions eleven times that Jesus prayed. Mark tells us in his very first chapter, "In the morning, rising up a great while before day, He went out, and departed into a solitary place and there prayed." Before He chose His twelve disciples "He went out into a mountain to pray, and continued all night in prayer to God." Such actions seem to have deeply impressed the disciples, as John used the significant expression, "He departed into a mountain *Himself alone."* Matthew also had written, "He went up into a mountain apart to pray, and when the even was come, *He was there alone."* Jesus Christ, as the perfect man, felt the need of complete solitude. Let us try to find out what this means.

Himself alone. He was entirely by Himself, alone with Himself. We know how much contacts with people draw us away from ourselves and exhaust our energy. The man Christ Jesus knew this too, and felt the need to be alone and gather all His powers to renew the consciousness of what He was and what He needed. He needed reaffirming from God for His high destiny, His human weakness, and His entire dependence upon the Father.

How much more does the child of God need this! Whether we are surrounded by the distractions of worldly pursuits or in the midst of service for the Lord, whether we need to maintain our own Christian life or renew our power to influence men for God, there is always the urgent call to come apart alone. We need to follow in our Master's steps and find the place and the time where we can indeed be alone with ourselves.

Himself alone, with spiritual realities. We need an entire withdrawal from the things which are seen and temporal so that we are free to yield ourselves fully to the powers of the unseen world and allow them to master us. Jesus needed fresh times to be quiet and realize the power of the kingdom of darkness with which He had come to contend and to conquer. He needed to contemplate the need of this great world of mankind which He had come to save, and get in touch with the presence and the power of the Father whose will He had come to do. The most indispensable thing in Christian service is that a person should at times set himself wholly apart to think intensely on the spiritual realities with which he is so familiar and yet has so often little grasped and exercised. The truths of eternity have an infinite power but they are often so powerless because we do not give them time to reveal themselves. Solitude is the only solution.

Himself alone, with God the Father. It is sometimes said that work is worship and that service is fellowship. If ever there were a man who could dispense with special times for solitude and fellowship, it was our Lord. But He showed us that He could not do His work or maintain His fellowship in full power without His quiet time. He felt the need, as a man, to bring all His work, past and future, before the Father. He needed to renew His sense of absolute dependence on the Father's power and absolute confidence in the Father's love with times of special fellowship. When He said, "the Son can do nothing of Himself," "as I hear so I speak," He was expressing the simple truth of His relation to God. It was this that made His going apart a necessity and an unspeakable joy.

I wish that every servant of the Lord understood and practiced this truth. I wish that the Church knew how to train believers into some sense of this high and holy privilege. Every believer not only may, but *must* have his time when he is himself alone with God. Oh! what a wonderful thought to have God all alone to myself, and to know that God has me alone to Himself!

Himself alone, with the Word. Our Lord as a man had to learn God's Word as a child. During the long years of His life in Nazareth, He fed on that Word and made it His own. In His solitude, He communed with the Father on all that that Word had spoken of Him, on all the will of God it revealed for Him to do.

In the Christian life, one of the deepest lessons to learn is that the Word without the living God does not count for much. The blessing of the Word comes when it brings us directly to the living God. Only the Word that we get from the mouth of God brings the power to know it and to do it. Let us learn the lesson well that personal fellowship with God alone in secret can make the Word come alive in power.

Himself alone, in prayer. Prayer allows a person to lay open his whole life to God and to ask for His teaching and His strength. What an unspeakable privilege that is! Think for a moment what prayer meant to Jesus, what adoring worship, what humble love, what childlike pleading for all He needed. Although we can't really grasp all of this, we can realize what a blessing waits for the man who knows how to follow in Christ's steps. God is waiting to do wonderful things for the one who makes this secret fellowship his chief joy.

Himself alone. Those words open to us the secret of the life of Christ on earth, and of the life that He now lives in us, by the Holy Spirit.

34

THE POWER OF INTERCESSION

"Tell me where your great strength lies," is the question we would like to ask of men of former times, and later times, who were such powerful intercessors. Many who have sincerely wanted to give themselves to the ministry of intercession have wondered why it is so difficult to find joy in it, to persevere, and to obtain results. Let us study the lives of the leaders and heroes of the prayer world to discover some of the elements of their success.

The true intercessor is a man who knows that God knows his heart and life are *wholly given to God for His glory*. This is the only condition on which an officer at the court of an earthly ruler could expect to exert much influence. Moses, Elijah, Daniel, and Paul proved that it is the same in the spiritual world. Our Lord Himself is also proof of it. He did not save us by intercession, but by self-sacrifice. His power of intercession claims and receives what the sacrifice won. Isaiah 53 put it so clearly, "He *poured out His soul unto death,* and was numbered with the transgressors, and He bare the sins of many, and..."—study this in connection with the whole chapter of which it is the climax— "*and made intercession* for the transgressors." He first gave Himself up to the will of God where He won the power to influence and guide that will. He gave Himself for sinners in all-consuming love, and so won the power to intercede for them. There is no other path for us. Whole-hearted devotion and obedience to God are the first marks of an intercessor.

You may complain that you do not feel able to pray that way, and ask how you may be fitted to do so. You may speak a lot about your weak faith in God, lack of love for souls, and little delight in prayer. The man who wants to have power in intercession must stop such complaints—he must realize that he has *a nature perfectly adapted to the work.* An apple tree is expected to bear only apples, because it has the apple nature within it. "You are God's workmanship, created in Christ Jesus unto good works." The eye was created to see: it is beautifully fitted for its work! You are created in Christ to pray. It is your very nature as a child of God. What has the Spirit been sent into your heart to do? To cry "Abba Father," and to draw your heart up in childlike prayer. The Holy Spirit prays in us with groanings that cannot be uttered, with a Divine power which our mind and feelings cannot understand. If you want to be an intercessor, learn to give the Holy Spirit much greater honor than is generally done. Believe that He is praying within you, and then be strong and of good courage. As you pray, be still before God to believe and yield to this wonderful power of prayer within you.

You may feel that there is so much conscious sinfulness and defect in your prayer. That may be true, but you must remember that you are to pray *in the name of Christ,* not your own name. That name means living power. Do you not know that you are in Christ and He is in you? That your whole life is hid and bound up in His, and His whole life is hid and working in you? The man who is to intercede in power must be very clear that in the most actual, living, Divine reality, *Christ and he are one in the work of intercession.* He appears before God clothed with the name and the nature, the righteousness and worthiness, the image and spirit and life of Christ. Do not spend most of your time in prayer repeating your petition, but humbly, quietly, confidently claiming your place in Christ, your perfect union with Him, your access to God in Him.

Intercession is pre-eminently a work of faith. Not the faith that only tries to believe that prayer will be heard, but the faith that is at home in heavenly realities. That kind of faith does not trouble about one's own nothingness and weakness, because it is living in Christ. That faith does not depend upon feelings, but upon the faithfulness of the Triune God, in what each Divine Person has undertaken to do in prayer. That faith has overcome the world, and sacrifices the visible so that it can be wholly free for the spiritual, heavenly, and eternal to take possession of it. That kind of faith knows that it is heard and receives what it asks. Therefore, it quietly and deliberately perseveres in its supplication until the answer comes. The true intercessor must be a man with that kind of faith.

The intercessor must be *a messenger*—one who holds himself ready, who earnestly offers himself personally to receive the answer and to dispense it. Praying and working go together. Think of Moses' boldness in pleading with God for the people and equally pleading with the people for God. We see the same in Elijah—the urgency of his prayer in secret is equaled by his jealousy for God in public, as he witnessed against the sin of the nation. Intercession should not be accompanied by more diligent work, but by waiting on God to know more definitely what and how He would have us work.

It is a great thing to begin to take up the work of intercession by which we draw down to earth the blessings from God for every need. It is a greater thing as an intercessor to personally receive that blessing and to go out from God's presence with something that we can give to others. May God make us all whole-hearted, believing, blessing-bearing intercessors.

35

THE INTERCESSOR

*"The effectual fervent prayer of a righteous
man availeth much. Elijah was a man subject to like passions as we are."*
(James 5:16,17)

The attitude that most weakens our desire to
follow in the steps of Scripture saints is to think
that they are exceptional cases and that what we see
in them is not to be expected of all. The aim of God
in Scripture is the very opposite! God has given
these men for our instruction and encouragement,
as examples of what His grace can do, as living
embodiments of what His will in our nature makes
possible.

That is just the reason James wrote, as an
encouragement to a life of effectual prayer, that
"Elijah was a man subject to like passions as we
are." Since there was no difference between his
nature and ours, or between the grace that worked
in him and that works in us, there is no reason why
we should not, like him, pray with effectiveness. If
our prayer is to have power, we must seek to have
some of Elijah's spirit. We should actually desire to
pray like Elijah. We need to seek for the secret of his
power in prayer. We shall find it in his life with

God, his work for God, and his trust in God.

Elijah lived with God. As a man lives, so he prays. I do not mean the words or thoughts which he has during set times of prayer, but the bent of his heart as seen in his desires and actions. That is regarded by God as his real prayer. The life speaks louder and truer than the lips. To pray well a man must live well. He who seeks to live with God will learn to know His mind and what gives Him pleasure to such an extent that he will be able to pray according to His will. Notice how Elijah, in his first message to Ahab, spoke of "the Lord God, before whom I stand." Think of his solitude at the brook Cherith, receiving his bread from God through the ravens, and then at Zarphath through the ministry of a poor widow. He walked with God and learned to know God well. When the time came, he knew how to pray to God whom he had proved. It is only out of a life of true fellowship with God that the prayer of faith can be born. Let the relationship between the life and the prayer be clear and close. As we give ourselves to walk with God, we shall learn to pray.

Elijah worked for God. He went where God sent him. He did what God commanded him. He stood up for God and His service. He witnessed against the people and their sin. All who heard him could say, "Now I know that thou art a man of God, and that the word of the Lord in thy mouth is truth." Elijah's prayers were all in connection with his work for God. He was a man of action and a man of prayer at the same time. When he prayed down the rain, after the drought, it was as part of his prophetic work so that the people by judgment and mercy might be brought back to God. When he prayed down fire from heaven on the sacrifice, it was that God might be known as the true God. His one motive was for the glory of God.

How often believers seek power in prayer so that they may be able to get good gifts for themselves. Secret selfishness robs them of the power and the answer. It is when self is lost in the desire for God's glory, and our life is devoted to work for God, that we will have the power to pray. God lives to love, save, and bless men. The believer who gives himself up to God's service will find new life in prayer. When we work for others, we prove that we are honest in our prayers for them. Work for God demonstrates both our need and our right to pray boldly. Cultivate the consciousness that you are wholly given up to His service. That will strengthen your confidence that He hears you.

Elijah trusted in God. He had learned to trust Him for his personal needs in the time of famine. He dared trust Him for greater things in answer to prayer for His people. Look at the confidence he had that God was hearing him and would do what he would ask. He dared to announce to Ahab that the rain was coming, and then, with his face to the ground, he pleaded for it, while his servant six times brought the message, "There is nothing." His unwavering confidence in the promise and character of God gave him power for the effectual prayer of the righteous man.

The inner chamber is the place where we have to learn that. The morning watch is the training school where we are to exercise the grace that can fit us to pray like Elijah. Let us not be afraid. The God of Elijah still lives; the Spirit that was in him dwells likewise in us. Let us stop talking about limited and selfish views of prayer, which only aim at grace enough to keep us standing. Let us cultivate the consciousness that Elijah had, that we can live wholly for God, and we can learn to pray like him. Prayer will bring to ourselves and to others a wonderfully new and blessed experience, that our prayers, too, are effectual and can result in great power.

Let us take courage and not be afraid in the power of that Redeeming Intercessor, who ever liveth to pray for us—the Holy Spirit. Have we given ourselves to God? Are we working for Him? Are we learning to know and trust Him? We can count on the life of God in us and the Holy Spirit dwelling in us, to lead us on to this grace. "The effectual prayer of the righteous man that availeth much."